The Medium and the Message

REAL POLITICS IN AMERICA

Series Editor: Paul S. Herrnson, *University of Maryland*

The books in this series bridge the gap between academic scholarship and the popular demand for knowledge about politics. They illustrate empirically supported generalizations from original research and the academic literature using examples taken from the legislative process, executive branch decision making, court rulings, lobbying efforts, election campaigns, political movements, and other areas of American politics. The goal of the series is to convey the best contemporary political science research has to offer in ways that will engage individuals who want to know about real politics in America.

THE MEDIUM AND THE MESSAGE
TELEVISION ADVERTISING AND AMERICAN ELECTIONS

EDITED BY

Kenneth M. Goldstein
University of Wisconsin–Madison

Patricia Strach
University of Wisconsin–Madison

UPPER SADDLE RIVER, NEW JERSEY 07458

Library of Congress Cataloging-in-Publication Data

The medium and the message: television advertising and American elections/edited by Kenneth M. Goldstein, Patricia Strach.—1st ed.
    p. cm.—(Real politics in America)
Includes bibliographical references and index.
  ISBN 0-13-177774-2
  1. Television in politics—United States—Congresses. 2. Television advertising—United States—Congresses. 3. Advertising, Political—United States—Congresses.
4. Elections—United States. I. Goldstein, Kenneth M. II. Strach, Patricia. III. Series.
  HE8700.76.U6M43 2003
    324.7'3'0973—dc22

                                                                                          2003021536

Editorial Director: Charlyce Jones Owen
Acquisitions Editor: Glenn Johnston
Assistant Editor: John Ragozzine
Editorial Assistant: Suzanne Remore
Director of Marketing: Beth Mejia
Marketing Assistant: Jennifer Bryant
Prepress and Manufacturing Buyer: Sherry Lewis
Interior Design: John P. Mazzola
Cover Design: Kiwi Design
Cover Photo: © AFP/Corbis
Composition/Full-Service Project Management: Kari Callaghan Mazzola and John P. Mazzola
Printer/Binder: Courier Companies, Inc.
Cover Printer: Phoenix Color Corp.

This book was set in 10/12 Palatino.

Real Politics in America
Series Editor: Paul S. Herrnson

Pearson Education LTD.
Pearson Education Singapore, Pte. Ltd
Pearson Education, Canada, Ltd
Pearson Education–Japan
Pearson Education Australia PTY, Limited

Pearson Education North Asia Ltd
Pearson Educación de Mexico, S.A. de C.V.
Pearson Education Malaysia, Pte. Ltd
Pearson Education, Upper Saddle River, NJ

10 9 8 7 6 5 4 3 2 1
ISBN 0-13-177774-2

To the Memory of Warren E. Miller

CONTENTS

PREFACE

The chapters in *The Medium and the Message: Television Advertising and American Elections* were originally presented at a conference in April 2001. The conference was attended by political scientists, journalists, consultants, and lawyers. This combination of campaign experts, who too often sit at separate intellectual and practical tables, was able to listen to and learn from each other in important ways. Our goal with this book is to build on the synergies at the conference, to communicate serious social science research on important policy issues to a wide variety of audiences, and to create a dialogue among scholars, journalists, and political professionals.

Generous grants from the Pew Charitable Trusts made this conference possible. More importantly, grants from the Trusts have made possible the purchase, processing, and analysis of content and targeting data on television advertising. These funds are not only allowing scholars and journalists to describe the nature of modern campaigns, but also allowing scholars to gauge their effectiveness. In the long term, these television advertising data will be a valuable archive for future scholars.

We would like to thank Evan Tracey, president of the Campaign Media Analysis Group, for making these data available to academics at a reasonable cost. His help and insight have made this project possible. We would also like to thank Michael Franz and Joel Rivlin for their excellent work as research assistants on all aspects of the project.

Without the help of all of these people the work of the Wisconsin Advertising Project would not be possible, and we are immensely grateful.

Kenneth M. Goldstein
Patricia Strach

THE MEDIUM AND THE MESSAGE

INTRODUCTION

KENNETH M. GOLDSTEIN AND PATRICIA STRACH

Television advertising is the primary means by which modern political campaigns communicate with potential voters. In a typical presidential, congressional, or gubernatorial election, spending on television advertising comprises the majority of a campaign's budget.

To date, the lack of comprehensive data on the content, timing, volume, and targeting of political advertising has limited what policymakers, journalists, and scholars can report about the strategies employed by campaigns and the balance of advertising in particular contests. Furthermore, the lack of comprehensive data on advertising activity by parties and interest groups—increasingly active players in advertising campaigns—not only has limited what could be said about the activities of these crucial players, but also has made it difficult to draw a complete picture of advertising activity. Finally, the lack of comprehensive data on political advertising has made it difficult for scholars to study the effect and effectiveness of these communications. Put simply, without comprehensive data on the targeting, volume, and content of advertising by all the players involved in federal campaigns, it has been difficult to study the nature of the main persuasive tool utilized by modern electoral campaigns.

A technology developed and marketed by Competitive Media Reporting (CMR) now tracks all advertising activity in the majority of the country (see <www.cmr.com>). The ad-tracking technology monitors the transmissions of the national networks (ABC, CBS, NBC, and Fox) as well as twenty-five national cable networks (such as CNN, ESPN, and TBS). More importantly, the system monitors local spot advertising in the country's top seventy-five media markets (comprising approximately 80 percent of the nation's population). The system's software recognizes the electronic seams between programming and advertising. When the system first detects a commercial spot's unique broadcast pattern, it downloads the ad and creates a storyboard (see following description and examples). Analysts code the advertisements into particular categories by product for commercial clients and by candidate or sponsor for political clients. The ads then are tagged with unique digital fingerprints. Thereafter, the system automatically recognizes and logs that particular commercial (or "creative") wherever and whenever it airs.

The ad-tracking technology is marketed and distributed to political clients by Campaign Media Analysis Group (CMAG). CMAG clients include both the Republican and Democratic National Committees, scores of congressional and gubernatorial campaigns as well as many prominent trade associations and interest groups (see <www.politicsontv.com>).

In 1998 and 2000, the data were purchased by the Brennan Center at New York University through a grant from the Pew Charitable Trusts. Once obtained, the data were processed and coded by teams of graduate and undergraduate students at the University of Wisconsin (2000) and Arizona State University (1998). For 1998, the CMAG data were purchased and coded after the election. In 2000, the data were purchased during the campaign and provided to the University of Wisconsin in real time, with much of the coding and processing occurring during the fall campaign in 2000. CMAG supplied two different forms of data that were used in this project. First, for every political ad produced, CMAG created a storyboard, including a complete transcript of all audio and a still capture of every fourth second of video. (Numerous examples of storyboards are included in the ensuing analysis.) These storyboards enabled us to undertake an extensive coding exercise. Specifically, a team of graduate and undergraduate students coded the content of each of these storyboards on a wide range of topics, ranging from the spot's main objective to its tone, the issues discussed, and even the characterizations used to describe candidates. The second type of CMAG data involved day-by-day reports on the targeting of all political ads in the nation's top seventy-five markets. The unit of analysis in these files was the broadcast of a unique spot. CMAG assigned a unique name to differentiate each ad, or creative, and then provided information on the time, length, station, show and estimated cost of each airing of the spot. For each ad, this frequency information was then merged with the coded content from the storyboards in order to produce the single, comprehensive data set of the Wisconsin Advertising Project (WiscAds).

With the ability to determine accurately the content of political advertising as well as how often, when, and where these ads were run, scholars are now able to test conventional wisdom and develop new hypotheses about electoral behavior and strategy. The researchers in this book address pressing questions facing scholars of American politics and citizens more generally: What motivates the use of campaign advertising, how effective is it, and how do party involvement and interest group involvement affect how candidates run their own races?

Outline for the Book

The first part of this book addresses the question of motivation: Why do parties, interest groups, or candidates air particular types of ads at particular times? Travis Ridout, Ken Goldstein, and Paul Herrnson show that ad sponsors engage in complex strategic behavior.

Travis Ridout, in Chapter 1, demonstrates that generalizations about motivation usually are based on *general* elections and a different set of norms exists in primaries. Ridout finds that specific characteristics of the primary election—their timing, their sequential nature, and their composition of multiple candidates in an intraparty contest—change the motivation of advertisers and leads to concrete differences from the general election in who sponsors ads, where they are aired, and the tone of the ads.

In Chapter 2, Ken Goldstein challenges conventional academic work that assumes that advertising effects are absent from presidential elections. Goldstein demonstrates with CMAG data and five case studies that even messages in *national* elections vary depending on the *local* market in which one lives.

Paul Herrnson, in Chapter 3, looks at what motivates issue advocacy by interest groups. Taking advantage of campaign finance laws that allow them virtually unlimited advertising for "issue advocacy," or ads that are targeted at issues rather than for or against a particular candidate, organizations have skirted the original intent of the laws by producing ads that serve the same purpose as electioneering, or promoting particular candidates. He suggests that far from the original intent of allowing unlimited issue advocacy, organized interests and political parties have cleverly targeted their message to do one thing: win elections.

The second part of this book addresses how effective advertising actually is, or more precisely, how individuals in the electorate respond to campaign advertising. Jonathan Krasno, in Chapter 4, questions whether or not issue advertising is as effective as money spent by the candidates themselves. The decision by advertisers to concentrate issue advertising in a limited number of races, ironically, makes such advertising less effective. Krasno finds that the overall impact of issue advertising was minimal in 1998 and 2000 except for a few key races.

In Chapter 5, David Magleby looks at whether outside "soft" money influences voters as effectively as regulated "hard" money. Using focus groups, surveys, and the targeting data from CMAG, Magleby concludes that voters often cannot tell the difference between party or interest group election ads and those run by the candidates themselves. Further, through monitoring campaign communications (such as mail), Magleby finds that outside money influences campaign strategy and agendas, making campaigns in competitive districts a team sport.

Paul Freedman and L. Dale Lawton, in Chapter 6, look specifically at the effectiveness of negative advertising. They propose a framework for studying advertising that takes into account viewer perception. Using an Internet ad test study coding and a survey panel study in addition to the CMAG frequency data, the authors show not all negative advertising is equally effective: Viewers react differently to ads depending on their judgments about whether the ads are honest, believable, or fair.

With campaign advertising it is tricky to address one particular actor in a campaign, such as a candidate, without also taking up interest groups and parties. All three play an important role in campaign advertising. CMAG data allow the authors in this book to analyze how candidates, parties, and interest groups differ in their strategies and even influence one another. Chapter 7, by David Parker and John Coleman, serves to put our work in this book into historical perspective. Parker and Coleman examine the ever-shifting balance between candidates, interest groups, and parties over time. The authors argue that the relationship between the three depends on resources necessary to win an election at any particular point in time. Detailing electoral and campaign finance laws over time, they show the relative power of one of the players with respect to the other two changes with institutional rules. They caution against any quick fixes to campaign problems because regulations that overwhelmingly affect one member of the triad inevitably opens up space for the other members to gain advantages.

Campaign Advertising Strategies in the 2000 Presidential Nominations

The Case of Al, George, Bill, and John

Travis N. Ridout[1]

The 2000 presidential primary season was the most fast-paced in the history of modern U.S. presidential nominations. Only six weeks after Iowa's January 24 caucuses, and only five weeks after New Hampshire's first-in-the-nation primary on February 1, Al Gore and George W. Bush secured the Democratic and Republican nominations respectively. During that short period of time, over twenty states had held either a presidential primary or caucus. It was truly a whirlwind campaign.

Yet there was also something rather "old-fashioned" about the 2000 presidential nomination campaign. In the present age, in which the big campaign story is often the tens of millions of dollars in soft money that parties and interest groups are spending to get candidates elected, the presidential primaries stand distinct. Indeed, the presidential primaries are one campaign context in which the candidates themselves—not parties or interest groups—take center stage in the running of the television campaign.

The evidence I present in this chapter suggests that the nomination campaign is still one in which candidates decide which issues to emphasize and how to present themselves in television advertising. That this should be so is not particularly surprising when one considers the unique features of the primary race—multiple candidates, sequential events, and intraparty competition, to name just a few. This chapter argues that the characteristics of the presidential nomination race influence campaign behavior in three important ways: who sponsors advertising, what its tone is, and where the advertising is aired.

The chapter proceeds as follows. Using advertising tracking data from the 2000 presidential nomination campaign, I first demonstrate the small role of groups as advertising sponsors in both the Republican and Democratic races. I then investigate the advertising strategies pursued by each of the candidates during the campaign, focusing on when and to what extent campaigns decided to "go negative." Finally, I turn attention to where geographically the campaigns decided to spend their resources on advertising and the potential impact of those decisions on citizen learning about the candidates.

WHO PLAYS THE PRIMARY ADVERTISING GAME?

In the general election presidential campaign, there are three sponsors of advertising: candidates, political parties, and interest groups. Yet not all three become involved in the primary race to the same degree. Like in the general election, candidates in primaries spend money on advertising for their own campaigns. But parties, because they are officially neutral in intraparty contests, tend to stay out of primary races. That leaves interest groups. Should we expect their investment in advertising to be as heavy in a primary campaign as it is in a general election? There are three reasons why this might not be the case. First, the policy differences among the viable candidates within a party are probably much smaller than the policy differences between the eventual nominees of the Republican and Democratic parties. As Magleby (2000) points out, groups would prefer to save their resources to oppose a real "enemy" in the general election rather than wasting them on opposing a less desirable but nonetheless acceptable candidate in the primaries.

Second, if a group is closely affiliated with one party, it may not want to risk offending that party's eventual nominee. Groups that want to work closely with one party need to be on good terms with whoever is nominated. Finally, on-the-ground involvement, such as door-knocking or setting up a phone bank, may be a better use of resources in some states. Because so few people vote in caucus states, ensuring that one's supporters show up to vote through ground efforts is more important than attempting mass persuasion through advertising. Similar logic applies in New Hampshire, which is ideally suited for a ground game. Because New Hampshire holds the nation's first primary, candidates have the time to set up on-the-ground operations. And because the state's population is relatively small, it is feasible to reach voters through individualized targeting rather than through mass media appeals.

The AFL-CIO's efforts on behalf of Al Gore in 2000 illustrate the point. Rather than spending money on television advertising (the union did not air any primary advertisements), the AFL-CIO distributed fliers to likely caucus attendees in Iowa and made personal visits and telephone contacts in New Hampshire (Sanders and Redlawsk 2000, Fowler, et al. 2000). My expectation, then, is that issue advocacy advertising will play a relatively small role in the primary campaign.

WHAT STRATEGIES DID THEY USE?

Journalistic accounts of presidential campaigns frequently adopt a conflict-ual frame, either to attract the attention of viewers or to make the story eas-ier to explain. It is not surprising, then, that public opinion surveys find that citizens view campaigns as being too negative and even downright nasty. In addition, the sheer volume of scholarly studies that examine the potential im-pact of negative campaign advertising on voter turnout, political efficacy, or affect toward a candidate leaves the impression that attack advertising is the norm. Indeed, Lau, et al. (1999) identified fifty-two studies, most from the mid- to late-1990s, in which negative advertising was the chief inde-pendent variable. However accurate this portrait of campaigns in general may be, it may be less apt a description of the primary season. In fact, some unique features of the primary race lead one to expect a fairly positive pri-mary campaign.

One thing that distinguishes a primary race from a general election is that there are usually more than two candidates competing. A candidate who wants to "go negative," then, must either design an advertisement that at-tacks all opponents, or choose to attack one opponent. The former strategy seems not only difficult to accomplish in a thirty-second advertisement, but invites reprisals from all directions. The latter strategy, attacking only one op-ponent, may serve only to benefit a third candidate in the race. A second dis-tinguishing feature of primaries is that they are intraparty contests, and party leaders are fearful of damaging the party's eventual nominee through a bruis-ing nomination contest. Although academic studies have had a difficult time establishing that divisive primaries do, in fact, hurt parties in November (Atke-son 1998), the conventional wisdom remains that divisive, negative primaries are damaging. Many Republicans were angered by Steve Forbes's attacks on Bob Dole during the 1996 primaries, a violation of the party's "11th Com-mandment" to never speak ill of a fellow Republican. Indeed, one group, the Republican Leadership Council, ran an advertisement in 2000 in which it ac-cused Forbes of having "a history of unfairly attacking fellow Republicans" and urged him to run a positive campaign.[2] My expectation is that primary candidates will stay relatively positive in their television advertising.

WHERE DO THEY ADVERTISE?

In deciding where to advertise, candidates must consider several features of the primary campaign that are not relevant in a general election, including sequential contests, multicandidate races and different methods of selecting delegates. These features suggest several expectations about the behavior of strategic politicians in the primaries.

1. Candidates are likely to advertise more in primaries that they have a chance of winning. One straightforward reason is that candidates will not want to waste money on primaries they are likely to lose. In this way, primary strategy is no different than a general election strategy in which a Democrat avoids competing in Utah and a Republican eschews Massachusetts. But what is different is the role of expectations. Since exceeding expectations is the name of the game in primaries (Bartels 1988), ensuring a good performance in primaries in which one is expected to do well is essential.

2. Candidates will tend to advertise more in primary than in caucus states. The media pay more attention to primary than to caucus results (Castle 1991), largely because primary results—which can be expressed in terms of votes rather than pledged delegates—are more easily interpreted for the public. Thus, spending the resources to win a primary rather than a caucus makes more sense. In addition, because turnout is much lower in caucuses than primaries, one gets more bang for the dollar by spending it in a primary state. And because caucus turnout is so low, those who do attend are reached more effectively through grassroots efforts than through the mass media.

3. Candidates are more likely to spend resources in states that hold their nomination events early. Doing well in an early primary has the potential to generate momentum for a candidate, much as it did for Jimmy Carter in 1976 or Gary Hart in 1984. A candidate who is unable to show some popular support in any early primary will likely have a hard time raising money from contributors and a hard time staying in the race as well.

4. Candidates will air more advertising in a state when the number of same-day nomination events is smaller. Financial resources constrain candidates' abilities to compete strongly in several states on the same day. They often must choose in which states they will compete and which states they will bypass.

5. Candidates are more likely to compete in states with a greater number of delegates.[3] For obvious reasons, acquiring more delegates enhances a candidate's chances of securing the party nomination, but winning a big state also demonstrates to the media and others that a candidate has the potential to do well among diverse constituencies, not just the stereotypical Iowa farmer or antitax citizen of New Hampshire.

I test these expectations using data obtained from the Campaign Media Analysis Group (CMAG). These data are described in the introduction to this book.

BACK TO THE VOTERS

Where candidates place their advertising certainly influences who wins the party nominations, but it matters as well for voter learning. Exposure to campaign advertisements can contribute to voter learning about the candidates

(Patterson and McClure 1976; Zhao and Chaffee 1995), and in consequence, informed choice in the voting booth. Yet many voters and state party officials complain that only a few states experience a "real" primary campaign nowadays; the rest of the country is ignored. They long for the "good old days" of 1972, when Democrats George McGovern and Hubert Humphrey were still competing for delegates in June, or 1976, when Republicans Ronald Reagan and Gerald Ford battled for the nomination up through the convention.

One unambiguous culprit for the change in the length of campaigns is front-loading—the increasing concentration of primary events in the early days of the primary season. Yet some scholars question how much voters actually learn about the candidates in a front-loaded campaign. Norrander, for one, argues that multistate primary dates and the compression of the primary calendar, both consequences of front-loading, "leave candidates with few opportunities for extensive campaigning in any state. Voters...will have little time to process the news about one event before the next occurs" (2000, p. 1000). In essence, Norrander is saying that today's campaigns do a poor job of educating voters.

Think a moment about what pattern of advertising would help to maximize voter learning about the candidates. First, it seems there would be substantial attention paid to all states during the primary campaign. The simple logic here is that more information contributes to more learning. Indeed, hotly contested campaigns—those featuring a lot of media coverage and television advertising—can reduce voter ambiguity about the candidates (Franklin 1991).

Second, one would want to see balanced advertising; that is, all candidates would air a similar number of advertisements. When one candidate sends a substantial number of messages more than an opponent, then citizens may have a hard time making an informed assessment of what the candidate positions are. For a person's political predispositions and vote choice to come into alignment, it is important that campaigns be balanced (Gelman and King 1993).

Finally, in order to aid voter learning, one would want to see advertising spread out over more than a day or two. To use an extreme example, seeing 100 campaign commercials in one week is likely to contribute more to a voter's knowledge than seeing those same 100 spots all on the day before the election. Having them spaced out may give voters the time to think about and process what they have seen. There is some evidence for this proposition in the marketing literature (Singh and Mishra 1994).

THE 2000 CAMPAIGN

The first nomination events, the Iowa caucuses, were held January 24, 2000—just six weeks before the race was effectively over.[4] Table 1.1 (on page 10) lists in chronological order the dates of all state primaries and caucuses until

TABLE 1.1   2000 PRIMARY SEASON

	REPUBLICAN	DEMOCRAT
Alaska	*Jan. 24*	
Iowa	*Jan. 24*	*Jan. 24*
New Hampshire	Feb. 1	Feb. 1
Hawaii	*Feb. 7–13*	
Delaware	*Feb. 8*	Feb. 5
South Carolina	Feb. 19	
Michigan	Feb. 22	
Arizona	Feb. 22	
Nevada	*Feb. 23*	
North Dakota	*Feb. 29*	
Washington	Feb. 29	Feb. 29*
Virginia	Feb. 29	
California	Mar. 7	Mar. 7
Connecticut	Mar. 7	Mar. 7
Georgia	Mar. 7	Mar. 7
Hawaii		*Mar. 7*
Maine	Mar. 7	Mar. 7
Maryland	Mar. 7	Mar. 7
Massachusetts	Mar. 7	Mar. 7
Minnesota	*Mar. 7*	
Missouri	Mar. 7	Mar. 7
New York	Mar. 7	Mar. 7
North Dakota		*Mar. 7*
Ohio	Mar. 7	Mar. 7
Rhode Island	Mar. 7	Mar. 7
Vermont	Mar. 7	Mar. 7
Washington		*Mar. 7*
South Carolina		Mar. 9
Colorado	Mar. 10	Mar. 10
Utah	Mar. 10	Mar. 10

Note: Italicized entries indicate caucuses.
*Non-binding
Source: Based on data from *CQ Weekly*, January 1, 2000, p. 25.

March 7. On the Democratic side, Vice President Al Gore picked up a healthy victory over his only opponent, former New Jersey Senator Bill Bradley, in Iowa. Among the Republicans, Texas Governor George W. Bush came out on top, beating Steve Forbes, Alan Keyes, and Gary Bauer. But Bush's strongest opponent, Arizona Senator John McCain, sat out the Iowa race. Just one week later New Hampshire held its primary. There Bradley showed some signs of life, managing to come within four percentage points of Gore. But the media story that night was John McCain's healthy victory over George W. Bush. McCain picked up 48 percent of the vote, compared to 30 percent for Bush, and in the eyes of the press became the new Gary Hart, the 1984 candidate who almost rode a wave of momentum to the Democratic nomination.

Delaware followed, holding its Democratic primary on February 5 and its Republican primary on February 8. Gore pulled out a victory there with 57 percent of the vote, but on the Republican side, Bush won, carrying 51 percent of the vote. He was followed by McCain with 25 percent and Forbes with 20 percent. Then the Republicans turned their attention to the South Carolina primary, which was held February 19. There Bush wound up the victor, gaining 53 percent of the vote to McCain's 42 percent.

While the Democrats were resting, Republicans prepared for the Michigan and Arizona contests, which were held three days after South Carolina, on February 22. McCain, as expected, handily won his home state of Arizona, but he surprised Bush with a victory in Michigan, thanks in large part to crossover voters, whom Bush accused of "trying to hijack the election" (Johnson 2000). The next Democratic contest after Delaware's February 5 primary was on February 29 in Washington state. Bradley, who believed winning the state was crucial for him to gain momentum, was defeated 68 to 31 percent by Gore. That same day Republicans competed in Washington, North Dakota, and Virginia. Bush won all three nomination events.

March 7, Super Tuesday, was do or die for the candidates. On that day, Gore swept all twelve Democratic nomination events, and Bush won eight of twelve Republican events. McCain's four victories came in the Northeast, in Rhode Island, Vermont, Massachusetts, and Connecticut. For McCain and Bradley, March 7 was the end of the road, and each pulled out of the nomination race days later. In just six weeks, Americans had selected their presidential nominees.

CANDIDATES AND GROUPS

Both academics and journalists have rightly focused on the prominent advertising role that interest groups played in the 2000 general election. It might be surprising to learn, then, that these groups were largely absent from the airwaves during the primary season. The number of spots aired by groups that implicitly supported or opposed a certain candidate—so-called "electioneering issue advocacy"—paled in comparison to the number of spots run by candidates themselves. From October 4 to March 15, only 2,470 electioneering issue-advocacy spots ran, compared to 61,433 hard money spots run by candidates (Table 1.2, page 12). Bush was the only candidate to receive considerable help from outside interest groups. Among those 2,470 spots, 1,722 were pro-Bush advertisements paid for by Republicans for Clean Air and run in

TABLE 1.2   COUNT AND COST OF SPOTS BY SPONSOR

	COUNT	COST
Candidate Ads		
Bush	23,959	$15,646,052
McCain	14,419	9,044,269
Bradley	11,267	11,219,799
Gore	7,953	7,843,769
Forbes	3,160	1,727,997
Bauer	435	103,560
Keyes	240	84,540
Candidate Subtotal	61,433	$45,669,986
Electioneering Issue Ads		
Pro-Bush	1,722	$1,355,679
Anti-Forbes	317	102,897
Anti-Bush	157	98,144
Anti-Gore & Bradley	92	55,465
Other	182	76,454
Electioneering Subtotal	2,470	$1,688,639
Grand Total	**63,903**	**$47,358,625**

Source: Based on data from Wisconsin Advertising Project.

New York, Ohio, and California during the week before the three states' March 7 primaries. Republicans for Clean Air, contrary to the name, was not a group of GOP identifiers concerned about air pollution, but rather a front for Sam Wyle, a wealthy supporter of George W. Bush (Dwyre, et al. 2001). The organization spent $1.35 million on television advertisements that attacked John McCain's environmental record and praised Bush's environmental efforts in Texas.

The Republican candidates aired almost 23,000 more spots than the Democrats, 42,213 to 19,220. There are several reasons the Republicans dominated the airwaves. One is that Republicans held more early primaries, such as those in South Carolina and Virginia. Democrats in those states did not choose a nominee until later. Second, while both Democrats accepted federal matching funds and thus had to abide by spending limits in each state, Republicans Bush and Forbes did not. Finally, there were more Republican candidates than Democrats, though this was not a major factor in the discrepancy; Bush and McCain accounted for over 91 percent of the Republican total.

The Bush campaign ran 23,959 spots, more than Gore and Bradley combined (Table 1.2). McCain ran more spots (14,449) than either Democrat did, but the Arizona Senator still fell far behind Bush in terms of the sheer volume of advertising. There was also an imbalance in the number of spots the two Democratic contenders ran. Incumbent Vice President Al Gore ran fewer spots (7,953) than did challenger Bill Bradley (11,267) in the seventy-five media markets examined.

The story is similar in terms of candidate spending, as shown by Table 1.2. Bush spent at least two-thirds more than McCain on television advertising, $15.6 million to $9.0 million. Bradley also outspent Gore, $11.2 million to $7.8 million. One cautionary note: These figures are surely underestimated as they include spending in only the seventy-five largest media markets, and do not include spending on ad production or distribution.

How (Fairly) Nice They Were

During the 2000 primary season, the dictum to speak well of fellow partisans was followed fairly well by candidates of both parties. A full 79 percent of the campaign commercials aired by candidates were positive, doing nothing more than saying nice things about that candidate without mentioning an opponent (Table 1.3, page 14). In terms of sheer volume of advertisements, Bush engaged in the most attack advertising. His campaign aired 2,067 attack spots, which represents 9 percent of the total spots that his campaign aired.

Bush stayed positive through Iowa and New Hampshire but began airing negative advertisements in South Carolina on February 4, two weeks before the state's Republican primary. It was by far the nastiest two weeks of the campaign. Bush's first ad charged rival John McCain with distorting Bush's tax plan. It also stated that McCain's chief economic adviser supported Bush's plan, a claim that drew the ire of McCain.

McCain responded three days later with two advertisements. The first accused Bush of breaking a promise to run a clean campaign. It asked, "Do we want another politician in the White House we can't trust?" The second was even more explicit in its mention of the incumbent president, saying that Bush's advertisement "twists the truth like Clinton." Bush's communications director, Karen Hughes, called the advertisements "offensive," while Bush spokesperson Ari Fleischer said it was "a disservice to our party and our principles" (Hotline 2000). Yet such rhetoric did not stop Bush from launching his own new attacks just one day later on February 8. The Bush advertisement stated: "McCain solicits money from lobbyists with interests before his committee and pressures agencies on behalf of contributors." On February 10, McCain responded with an advertisement that criticized Bush for running a negative campaign, airing it 333 times in South Carolina.

In the midst of the nastiness on television, there were allegations and counterallegations of push polling and a row about a Bush surrogate who said McCain had abandoned veterans. But by the 14th, McCain had returned to running a positive campaign, fearing that his image of a reformer might be

TABLE 1.3   NUMBER OF SPOTS BY SPONSOR AND TONE

	ATTACK	CONTRAST	PROMOTE	ALL ADS
Candidate Ads				
Bush	2,067	5,508	16,384	23,959
McCain	38	3,859	10,522	14,419
Bauer		148	287	435
Forbes	22	367	2,771	3,160
Keyes			240	240
Gore		1	7,952	9,753
Bradley		873	10,394	11,267
Count within candidate ads	2,127	10,756	48,550	61,433
Percent within candidate ads	3%	18%	79%	100%
Electioneering Ads				
Pro-Bush		1,722		1,722
Anti-Forbes	317			317
Anti-Bush	149	8		157
Anti-Gore & Bradley	92			92
Other	182			182
Count within electioneering ads	740	1,730	0	2,470
Percent within electioneering ads	30%	70%	0%	100%
Total Count	**2,867**	**12,486**	**48,550**	**63,903**
Total Percent	**4%**	**20%**	**76%**	**100%**

Source: Based on data from Wisconsin Advertising Project.

sullied. Bush continued to run a largely negative contrast advertisement until the February 19 primary. It is clear that campaigning in South Carolina was by far the nastiest of the nomination race. Still, over two-thirds of the candidate advertisements run in the state over the course of the campaign were purely positive.

Although coders identified few attack advertisements, they did find a larger number of contrast advertisements—those that seek to make distinctions between a candidate and an opponent. Eighteen percent of candidate spots aired sought to make contrasts between a candidate and an opponent. In truth, contrast advertisements range considerably in their tone (Freedman and Lawton 2002). Some resemble positive advertisements in that they stick to a comparison of issues, not character or personality, and they may only refer to a candidate's opponent generically, not mentioning him or her by name. On the other hand, some contrast advertisements are barely distinguishable from attack advertisements in that the bulk of the commercial may speak of an opponent by name in a negative tone. In order to obtain conservative estimates about how positive the candidate advertisements were, I focus my analysis on the percent of each candidate's advertisements that were clearly positive.

The two Democrats were more cordial than their Republican counterparts. Ninety-three percent of the spots aired by Bill Bradley were positive ones promoting his candidacy. Al Gore aired only one advertisement that even mentioned Bill Bradley, and it aired exactly once. On the Republican side, Alan Keyes was the most positive candidate, airing no negative or contrast advertisements. Gary Bauer was slightly more negative. Sixty-six percent of his spots promoted himself; the remainder contrasted his policies on national security with those of his Republican opponents. But both Keyes's and Bauer's airtime was miniscule compared with that of McCain and Bush. In that matchup, McCain was slightly more positive. Seventy-three percent of McCain's television spots were positive, while 68 percent of Bush's advertisements were. Steve Forbes, though his advertisements were 88 percent positive, was the first candidate of the race to run an advertisement that mentioned an opponent. Forbes's ad, which first ran November 24 in Iowa, attacked Bush for not repudiating an ad run on Bush's behalf by the Republican Leadership Council. The RLC ad to which Forbes was referring was launched eight days earlier in Iowa and New Hampshire and resurrected complaints about negative advertising Forbes had aired during his 1996 campaign.

Forbes attacked again in early January with an advertisement that accused Bush of violating a "no new taxes" pledge while Texas governor. That same day, the Republican Leadership Council, a Republican group, began airing spots that said that Forbes's advertisement "distorts the truth." The spot also suggested to viewers that Forbes's going negative might help Democrats in the long run by damaging Bush.

Gore was slower to respond to Bradley when the latter spent over $500,000 on two advertisements in mid-February that questioned Gore's commitment to abortion rights and gun control. These were aired in several states holding March 7 primaries, but the plurality of spots ran in Washington state, which voted a week before Super Tuesday and where Bradley hoped to gain some momentum. Gore did not counter with his own advertisement on the subject until March 5 in New York. It was the same nonpositive advertisement mentioned earlier that aired only once. Gore's advertisement was apparently designed for the consumption of the news media rather than voters.

Much of the campaign's dirty work was left to outside groups. Not a single electioneering issue advocacy advertisement was positive; all were coded contrast or attack. Anti-McCain groups (which are virtually synonymous with pro-Bush groups) were the most active in the campaign, airing 1,825 spots. The Republicans for Clean Air advertisement, which was mentioned earlier, attacked John McCain's environmental record while extolling that of Bush. This advertisement accounted for most of the outside help that Bush received, airing 1,722 times in Ohio, California, and New York. Another advertisement from the National Smoker's Alliance, though it did not specifically mention

Bush, criticized John McCain for supporting "the largest consumer tax increase in history," apparently a reference to the cigarette tax. The advertisement, which aired only thirty-two times, was seen in Michigan and Virginia. Another anti-McCain advertisement ran in South Carolina. Voters for Campaign Truth, echoing some of the arguments of the Christian Coalition, used the words of Warren Rudman, one of McCain's campaign chairmen, to question McCain's commitment to the anti-abortion position. The advertisement urged McCain to stop his "bigoted attack on the Christian voters of South Carolina and America."

In summary, television advertising in the 2000 nomination campaign resembled that of an "old-fashioned" campaign in that the candidates themselves dominated the advertising and that advertising was, on the whole, quite positive. If the role played by outside interest groups in the primary campaign were to grow in the future, however, then one might expect campaigns to become more negative, as electioneering issue advocacy was consistently more negative than campaign advertisements. Yet that is far from certain given the various disincentives for group participation in the primaries outlined previously.

HOW GEOGRAPHY MATTERED

In an earlier section of this chapter, I listed five expectations about where candidates would focus their advertising activities. Here I investigate whether those expectations were correct.

1. Candidates will spend more in states that they have a chance of winning. There is some evidence for this proposition.[5] For instance, Bill Bradley spent almost $500,000 in Washington State, more than he spent in all but three other states, first-in-the-nation New Hampshire, and mega-states California and New York (Table 1.4, page 18). In terms of number of advertisements, Bradley aired more in only those three states and Iowa (Table 1.5, page 19). Washington, a relatively liberal state, was a state that Bradley believed he could win. Moreover, Bush did not make an effort in the four New England states holding March 7 primaries, preferring to put his money into states where his conservative message would have more traction. One anomaly, however, was Bush's heavy spending in Arizona, McCain's home state. Most likely, Bush wanted to make McCain vulnerable, hoping that a better-than-expected showing there might garner him some positive media attention and generate doubts about McCain's popularity.

2. Candidates, as expected, aired more spots in states that held primaries rather than caucuses. Four states holding nomination events on March 7 or before held caucuses; unfortunately, CMAG data cover media markets in only two of those: Iowa and Minnesota.[6] Iowa received considerable candidate attention, but it did not match that heaped on New Hampshire, which voted just

one week later. While Iowa stations aired 5,324 spots, New Hampshire stations aired 11,961.[7] Minnesota received a paltry 11 candidate spots, all run by the Bradley campaign. Comparably sized primary states, however, received much more advertising. Maryland stations, for instance, aired 726 spots, and Missouri stations aired 494 spots.

3. A third expectation was that states holding early nomination events would receive more advertising. This certainly appears to be true, as Iowa, New Hampshire, and South Carolina—three of the first four states to hold nomination events—all received considerably more advertising than one might expect based on their small sizes.[8]

4. It was also suggested that candidates would be stingier with advertising expenditures within a state that holds its primary on the same day as many other states. Some of this appears to have happened on March 7, the day thirteen states held nomination events. All candidates bypassed Georgia, a state that offered a fairly large number of delegates to the victor, and only Bradley showed any effort in Minnesota. As noted earlier, Bush aired no advertisements in the four New England states voting that day. Gore was a no-show in Ohio.

5. Finally, large states, with their large number of delegates, experienced considerably more advertising than did small states. California and New York were tops in terms of the number of advertisements aired. Part of this is undoubtedly a function of these states being large geographically and having more media markets. Nonetheless, the average number of advertisements per media market was still much greater in these states than in smaller states, with a few exceptions. If one looks at all of the Super Tuesday states, highlighted in Table 1.6 (page 20), one sees that the three largest among them—California, New York, and Ohio—were among the top four in terms of the number of advertisements aired in each media market. Smaller states are grouped in the bottom half of the list.

The analysis presented here about the reasons candidates choose to go on the air in certain places is admittedly only suggestive as it is difficult to sort through the many factors that potentially contribute to decisions about where to place advertising. A multivariate regression analysis might be better able to sort out the impact of each predictor of advertising involvement, but unfortunately, the small number of states in the population makes this approach unfeasible.

WHAT DID VOTERS RECEIVE?

As argued previously, for primary voters to make informed decisions about the candidates, one would want to see substantial campaigning in all states. Was this the case in 2000? Returning to Table 1.6 (page 20), one sees the average number of candidate and electioneering issue advertisements run in each

TABLE 1.4 AD SPENDING BY SPONSOR AND STATE

	BUSH	MCCAIN	BAUER	FORBES	KEYES	GORE	BRADLEY	GROUPS	TOTAL
Arizona	$1,230,072			$87,087				$36,669	$1,353,828
California	$2,840,685	$2,384,748				$2,593,660	$3,315,499	$220,325	$11,354,917
Colorado	$417	$100,969							$101,386
Connecticut						$143,008	$150,038		$293,046
D.C.								$15,263	$15,263
Florida		$624					$3,650		$4,274
Illinois							$26,093		$26,093
Iowa	$339,089		$96,432	$434,973	$10,387	$295,710	$407,792	$23,177	$1,607,560
Kansas		$245							$245
Maine						$33,428	$66,932		$100,360
Maryland	$85,846	$72,115				$162,191	$216,366		$536,518
Massachusetts						$121,784	$233,744		$355,528
Michigan	$2,452,774	$1,430,318						$3,986	$3,887,078
Minnesota							$10,283		$10,283
Missouri	$80,586	$70,759				$100,917	$142,973		$395,235
New Hampshire	$3,060,337	$1,987,998	$7,128	$1,199,716	$60,400	$2,550,245	$3,895,959	$220,791	$12,982,574
New Mexico		$185							$185
New York	$476,178	$387,546				$1,398,404	$2,150,050	$998,766	$5,410,944
Ohio	$816,666	$721,168					$20,346	$159,517	$1,717,697
Rhode Island		$341				$24,094	$85,584		$110,019
South Carolina	$977,160	$772,902		$6,221	$13,493			$7,871	$1,777,647
Tennessee		$298							$298
Texas		$254							$254
Utah					$260				$260
Virginia	$1,827,793	$597,736					$8,383	$2,274	$2,436,186
Washington	$1,458,449	$516,063				$420,328	$486,107		$2,880,947
Total	**$15,646,052**	**$9,044,269**	**$103,560**	**$1,727,997**	**$84,540**	**$7,843,769**	**$11,219,799**	**$1,688,639**	**$47,358,625**

Source: Based on data from Wisconsin Advertising Project.

Table 1.5 Number of Spots Aired by Sponsor and State

	Bush	McCain	Bauer	Forbes	Keyes	Gore	Bradley	Other	Total
Arizona	1,425			82				53	1,560
California	2,478	2,474				1,989	2,644	164	9,749
Colorado	2	119							121
Connecticut						178	278		456
D.C.								24	24
Florida		1					10		11
Illinois							16		16
Iowa	1,192		420	1,290	41	976	1,287	118	5,324
Kansas		1							1
Maine						78	210		288
Maryland	99	73				216	338		726
Massachusetts						92	196		288
Michigan	3,910	2,680						17	6,607
Minnesota							11		11
Missouri	104	72				158	160		494
New Hampshire	2,801	1,854	15	1,771	136	2,340	2,570	474	11,961
New Mexico		1							1
New York	1,312	995				1,236	2,441	1,343	7,327
Ohio	1,528	1,286					44	244	3,102
Rhode Island		1				52	313		366
South Carolina	2,729	2,249		17	62			13	5,070
Tennessee		1							1
Texas		1							1
Utah					1				1
Virginia	3,753	1,492					9	20	5,274
Washington	2,626	1,119				638	740		5,123
Total	23,959	14,419	435	3,160	240	7,953	11,267	2,470	63,903

Source: Based on data from Wisconsin Advertising Project.

TABLE 1.6   AVERAGE NUMBER OF SPOTS
PER MEDIA MARKET IN EACH STATE

STATE	NUMBER OF SPOTS
New Hampshire	6,269
Iowa	2,662
Washington	2,562
South Carolina	2,535
Michigan	2,202
California	**1,950**
Arizona	1,560
New York	**1,465**
Virginia	1,258
Maryland	**726**
Ohio	**620**
Connecticut	**456**
Rhode Island	**366**
Massachusetts	**288**
Missouri	**247**
Colorado	121
Maine	**31**
Illinois	16
Florida	11
Minnesota	**11**
Kansas	1
Utah	1
Tennessee	1
Texas	1
New Mexico	1

Note: Super Tuesday states highlighted in bold.
Source: Based on data from Wisconsin Advertising Project.

market in each state. If one uses the rather arbitrary cutoff of 1,000 spots to distinguish states that received "substantial" attention from those that did not, then voters in nine states saw part of the campaign action. Lowering the cutoff point to 100 spots results in seven more states being added to the roster. Of course, the number of spots aired does not measure the time that candidates spent on the stump in a locale, but it does serve as a good indicator of how active candidates were in a state.

It is difficult to know the intensity of campaigning that is necessary to facilitate voter learning, but it is probably safe to say that more messages—and from a variety of candidates—are better. If nothing else, the evidence here suggests substantial variation across states in the number of candidate communications to which voters are exposed.

What about the balance of coverage? Figure 1.1 depicts spending by the two Democratic candidates in each primary. Although Bradley slightly outspent Gore in each nomination event, candidate spending was fairly well balanced in each state. Except for Massachusetts and Rhode Island, where Bradley at least doubled Gore spending, the discrepancies between the two candidates were not great, with New Hampshire a possible exception. In Washington state, for instance, Gore spent only about $60,000 less than Bradley did, and in Connecticut Bradley outspent Gore by only about $7,000.

On the Republican side, shown in Figure 1.2 on page 22 (Forbes, Bauer, and Keyes are dropped from the figure), the imbalances are much greater. McCain almost matched Bush's spending in South Carolina, with Bush spending only about $200,000 more than McCain—$977,160 to $772,902. No other candidate spent more than a few thousand dollars in the state. By the time Michigan's primary had arrived, however, McCain fell behind in spending and was considerably outspent in the two February 29 contests in Virginia and Washington. He was, however, able to come close to the amount spent by Bush in the Super Tuesday states. It is a mixed picture on the GOP side in terms of the balance of the advertising campaigns.

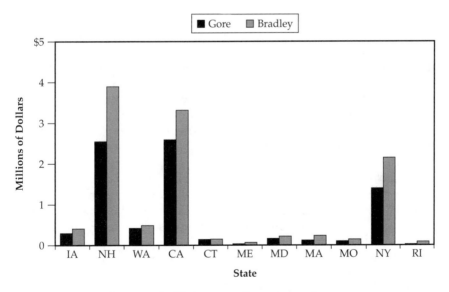

FIGURE 1.1   DEMOCRATIC SPENDING BY STATE

Note: States in which the two candidates combined spent less than $50,000 are eliminated from the figure.
Source: Based on data from Wisconsin Advertising Project.

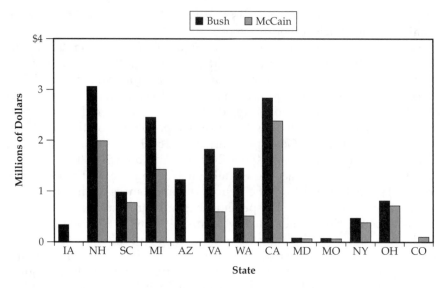

FIGURE 1.2   REPUBLICAN SPENDING BY STATE

Note: States in which the two candidates combined spent less than $50,000 are eliminated from the figure.
Source: Based on data from Wisconsin Advertising Project.

Turn now to how concentrated advertising was. One way to measure the concentration of a state's advertising is to calculate the cumulative percentage of a state's total advertising over the campaign that has aired by each day of the campaign. Figures 1.3a through 1.3f depict these calculations visually for several states chosen for the range of advertising concentration that they represent.

Figure 1.3a, for instance, reveals that the television campaign in New Hampshire continued rather steadily from late November to mid-February. There is no sign that the pace of advertising accelerated before the state's February 22 primaries. New Hampshire voters had a rather constant stream of candidate messages being sent to them—and over three months to sort through them. A full month before the vote, 32 percent of the total spots aired had already been aired. A similar pattern prevails in Michigan (Figure 1.3b), although there is more evidence of a stepped-up pace of advertising in the final two weeks of the campaign there. Virginia (Figure 1.3c) is almost identical to Michigan.

By contrast, advertising in the New York campaign (Figure 1.3d) is much more concentrated, beginning just two weeks before the vote, and spiking just days before the primary. In Ohio (Figure 1.3e), about 90 percent of the total spots aired in the state ran in the 10 days prior to the primary. Perhaps

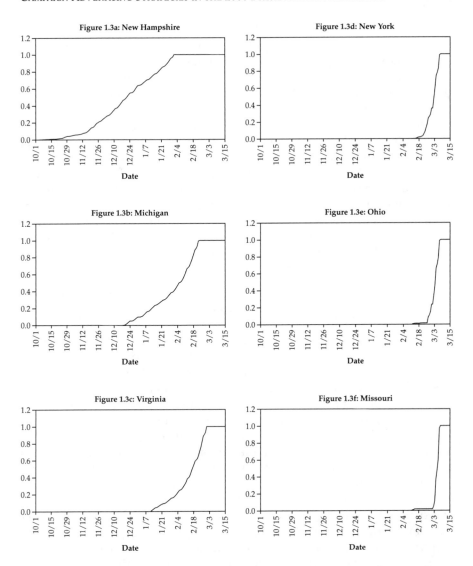

FIGURE 1.3A–F   CUMULATIVE PROPORTION OF SPOTS AIRED WITHIN A STATE BY DAY

Source: Based on data from Wisconsin Advertising Project.

the most concentrated television campaign took place in Missouri (Figure 1.3f), where 95 percent of the total spots were aired in the week before the March 7 primary. It is unlikely that voters in states like New York, Ohio, and Missouri had sufficient time to think through the various messages bombarding them.

This analysis points to a potentially important new variable in the investigation of voter learning during campaigns: the concentration of the messages sent. Yet the standard procedure in most studies is to include only the number of spots aired as a predictor variable. If one did that using these data, then Virginia and New York, for instance, would appear to have similar information environments as the average number of spots aired in each Virginia market—only slightly less than the average number in each New York market (1,258 versus 1,465). Yet if one takes into account the concentration of advertising, then the states look quite dissimilar, with Virginia receiving its advertising over the course of six weeks with New York receiving the bulk of its in only two. If voter learning truly is dependent on voters having sufficient time to process the messages they receive—not just their receiving a lot of messages—then candidates might consider spreading out their television campaigns over more than a few days. This assumes, of course, that candidates believe that a more knowledgeable electorate is beneficial to their electoral chances.

CONCLUSION

Presidential nomination campaigns are distinct from general election campaigns in many ways. Primaries are multicandidate events, pit copartisans against each other, and take place over the course of several weeks. Therefore, it is not surprising that many conclusions drawn about the role of television advertising in general election campaigns do not apply to nominations. In primaries, candidates still control the presentation of themselves through their television advertisements. Magleby and his colleagues (2000) are right to emphasize the involvement of outside groups in the campaign, but the amount that these groups spent on advertising is still only a fraction of what the candidates spent.

In contrast to popular perception, candidates themselves were overwhelmingly positive in their television advertising. This, however, is not all that surprising given the pressures facing candidates to refrain from attacking fellow partisans for fear of aiding the other party. As expected, candidates appear to focus their advertising efforts in states that vote earlier, in larger states, in states they expect to do well in, in states holding primaries rather than caucuses, and in states that are relatively isolated on the primary calendar. Finally, I speculated about some of the effects of these candidate advertising decisions on the ability of voters to become informed about the candidates. An important next step is to test empirically the relationship between the advertising behavior of candidates and voter learning in primaries. For instance, one could compare the volume, balance, and timing of candidate advertising with the amount and rate of voter learning in each state, presumably captured through public opinion data.

The chief message of this chapter is simple: Candidate strategy in presidential primaries, though it follows many of the generalizations that social scientists make about campaigns, also responds to the many rules of the game that make primaries unique. Thus, from a methodological standpoint, the study of primary campaigns provides important leverage in answering questions about the effects of institutions and structures on campaign behavior. But this study of the presidential primary campaign also serves as a caution against assuming that changes witnessed in congressional or presidential general elections are present in all other campaign contexts.

REFERENCES

Atkeson, Lonna Rae. "Divisive Primaries and General Election Outcomes: Another Look at Presidential Campaigns." *American Journal of Political Science* 42 (1998): 256–271.

Bartels, Larry M. *Presidential Primaries and the Dynamics of Public Choice.* Princeton, NJ: Princeton University Press, 1988.

Castle, David S. "Media Coverage of Presidential Primaries." *American Politics Quarterly* 19 (1991): 33–42.

Dwyre, Diana, Bruce Cain, Ray LaRaja, Joe Doherty, and Sam Kernell. "Outside Money in the California 2000 Presidential Primary." In *Getting Inside the Outside Campaign.* Ed. David Magleby. Center for the Study of Elections and Democracy, Brigham Young University, 2000.

Fowler, Linda L., Constantine J. Spiliotes, and Lynn Vavreck. "The Role of Issue Advocacy Groups in the New Hampshire Primary." In *Getting Inside the Outside Campaign.* Ed. David Magleby. Center for the Study of Elections and Democracy, Brigham Young University, 2000.

Franklin, Charles H. "Eschewing Obfuscation? Campaigns and the Perception of U.S. Senate Incumbents." *American Political Science Review* 85 (1991): 1193–1214.

Freedman, Paul, and Dale Lawton. 2002. Chapter 6 in this volume.

Gelman, Andrew, and Gary King. "Why Are American Presidential Election Campaign Polls So Variable When Votes are So Predictable?" *British Journal of Political Science* 23 (1993): 409–451.

Hotline, "Bushies Hit Back." *Hotline.* 8 February 2000.

Johnson, Glen. "Bush Tries to Rebound; Rips McCain over Dem 'Crossovers'." *Chicago Sun-Times.* (24 February 2000): Midwest Edition, 1.

Lau, Richard R., Lee Sigelman, Caroline Heldman and Paul Babbitt. "The Effects of Negative Political Advertisements: A Meta-Analytic Assessment." *American Political Science Review* 93 (1999): 851–875.

Magleby, David. 2002. Chapter 5 in this volume.

Magleby, David, ed. *Getting Inside the Outside Campaign.* Center for the Study of Elections and Democracy, Brigham Young University, 2000.

Norrander, Barbara. "The End Game in Post-Reform Presidential Nominations." *Journal of Politics* 62 (2000): 999–1013.

Patterson, Thomas E. and Robert D. McClure. *The Unseeing Eye: The Myth of Television Power in National Elections.* New York: G. P. Putnam's Sons, 1976.

Sanders, Arthur and David Redlawsk. "Money and the Iowa Caucuses." In *Getting Inside the Outside Campaign.* Ed. David Magleby. Center for the Study of Elections and Democracy, Brigham Young University, 2000.

Singh, Surendra N., and Sanjay Mishra. "Enhancing Memory of Television Commercials Through Message Spacing." *Journal of Marketing Research* 31 (1994): 384–392.

Zhao, Xinshu, and Steven H. Chaffee. "Campaign Advertisements Versus Television News As Sources of Political Issue Information." *Public Opinion Quarterly* 59 (1995): 41–65.

NOTES

1. Thanks to Ken Goldstein, Mike Franz, and Patricia Strach for very helpful comments on this chapter.

2. CMAG advertisement titled "RLC/At IT Again."
3. This may especially be true in states with winner-take-all delegate allocation.
4. The virtually ignored Alaska Republican caucuses were also held January 24.
5. All spots run in the Boston media market before the New Hampshire primary were credited to New Hampshire's total. After February 1, Boston spots were given to Massachusetts. Similarly, spots run in Portland, Maine, were credited to New Hampshire before February 1, spots run in the Charlotte, N.C., market before February 19 were given to South Carolina, spots run in Omaha before January 24 were given to Iowa, and spots run in Washington, D.C., before February 29 were credited to Virginia. In all other cases, the spots were assigned to the state in which the market's major city was located. So, for instance, spots airing in St. Louis were credited to Missouri, not Illinois.
6. North Dakota and Hawaii are the two other caucus states.
7. Some markets in each state are not covered by CMAG data, but the counts should be comparable nevertheless since almost all Iowa spots come from the Des Moines-Ames market and almost all New Hampshire spots come from the Boston market.
8. Delaware held its primaries between New Hampshire and South Carolina, but no Delaware stations are included in the CMAG data.

WHAT DID THEY SEE
AND WHEN DID THEY SEE IT?

MEASURING THE VOLUME, TONE, AND TARGETING
OF TELEVISION ADVERTISING
IN THE 2000 PRESIDENTIAL ELECTION

KENNETH M. GOLDSTEIN[1]

With a focus on the basic partisan and economic factors that drive presidential contests, scholars have usually discounted the potential effect of even large numbers of ads. Undoubtedly, such fundamental factors can explain most of the variance in presidential election outcomes. There is evidence, however, that advertising can matter at the margin—perhaps a few percentage points (Finkel 1993, Freedman and Goldstein 2000, Shaw 1999). And, in an election where thirteen states were decided by fewer than four percentage points and five states were virtual ties (Florida, Iowa, Oregon, New Mexico, and Wisconsin), might advertising have had a small effect in terms of actual voters influenced, but a big effect in influencing an entire election? Possibly. Yet, scholars have assumed that presidential contests, with their national tides, common strategic objectives, and relatively even resources, are not characterized by the kinds of one-sided information flows thought to be necessary for persuasive effects to be found and have typically considered presidential contests to be an especially poor place to search for advertising effects (Zaller 1992). But, do the actual data support scholarly assumptions discounting advertising effects in presidential elections? In this chapter, I suggest that there are important advertising effects in presidential elections when evaluated at the market rather than national level. In the first part, I use CMAG data to show that even though the two tickets and their party allies and interest group allies were evenly matched nationally, there was significant heterogeneity in the volume of the advertising from market to market. Relying on five case studies, in the second part I demonstrate that even in competitive markets the advertising patterns differed significantly.

Political Advertising in the 2000 Presidential Race

CMAG tracked 302,450 presidential spots in 2000. The vast majority of these spots (247,224) were aired after June 1 and were directed at the general election contest. (This figure includes ads aired by Nader, Buchanan, and other minor party candidates.) These quarter-million airings include not only the hard money ads sponsored by the campaign committees themselves, but coordinated expenditures with parties and soft money party ads, along with "issue advocacy" campaigns by interest groups. To put these 2000 presidential numbers in perspective, in four years there was a full 48 percent increase in the number of ads aired in the presidential race. (In 1996, the Clinton and Dole campaigns and their party and interest group allies aired 162,160 general election spots in the top seventy-five markets.)[2]

In terms of total spots aired in the presidential race, the Bush-Cheney ticket enjoyed a modest three-percentage-point lead in spots aired over the Gore-Lieberman forces (126,584 spots for Bush and his allies, 119,159 for Gore and his allies). Again, these numbers combine the different sources or sponsors of advertising in the presidential race—candidate, coordinated, party, and interest group—and it is important to note that each of the campaigns relied on different sponsors to varying extents. For example, over half the ads (52 percent) aired on behalf of Bush were paid for by the Republican National Committee. The Bush-Cheney campaign committee aired only one in five of the spots that were broadcast in support of the Republican ticket. Another 24 percent were aired in coordinated fashion using Republican hard money and funds from the campaign. Notably, interest groups were not particularly active on behalf of the GOP ticket in terms of the television air war. (Republican-leaning interest groups, were, however, big players in congressional contests). The story was much different on the Democratic side. Interest groups sympathetic to Gore and Lieberman aired 14 percent of all the ads that were broadcast in support of the Democratic ticket. The two biggest interest group supporters of the Gore campaign in terms of spot advertising were Planned Parenthood and the AFL-CIO. Party expenditures also dwarfed the amount spent by the actual campaign. The Democratic National Committee sponsored nearly half of the ads (48 percent) aired for the Democratic presidential ticket and the Gore-Lieberman campaign paid for about three in ten spots (31 percent).

Focusing on the competitive balance, at first glance, the modest three-percentage-point advantage by the Bush forces does not seem like particularly good news in the search for unbalanced flows of advertising. Furthermore, if one takes out the Bush campaign's decision to contest California, the national advertising numbers look virtually even. Nevertheless, the Bush buys in Los Angeles, San Diego, Sacramento, and Fresno are a reminder that one's attention must focus on markets in the search for advertising activity and advertising advantages.

When the unit of analysis is the market, a portrait of significant heterogeneity emerges. As was widely observed and reported during the 2000 contest, both sides pursued electoral college strategies that ignored markets that were safe for one side or the other and concentrated their resources on markets in swing states. Table 2.1 shows the markets where the ten most-intense advertising campaigns were waged in the presidential race. In general, both sides targeted the same markets. These choices demonstrate the importance of markets in Michigan, Missouri, New Mexico, Oregon, Pennsylvania, Washington, and Wisconsin in the 2000 presidential contest. On the other hand, major markets like Baltimore, New York, Dallas, and Houston received virtually no advertising in the presidential race. Chicago received some attention over the summer, but was ignored after Labor Day. Markets in New York, Texas, Illinois, and Maryland were simply not in play in the presidential race.

There were, however, some differences in targeting patterns. Table 2.2 (page 30) shows the top ten markets where the Republican ticket had an advantage in spots aired and Table 2.3 (page 30) lists the top ten markets where the Democratic ticket had an advantage in spots aired.

Assessing the exact nature of advantages in advertising can be a tricky exercise. Just looking at the lead that one side has in terms of number of spots (or any metric for that matter) can be misleading because a thousand-spot advantage in a market with relatively little advertising is likely to have a different effect than a thousand-spot advantage in a market that is being heavily targeted. In other words, just looking at spot advantages, hypothetical markets where Bush had a 1,000 to 0 advantage would look the same as a market where Bush had a 2,000 to 1,000 advantage or a 7,000 to 6,000 advantage. On

TABLE 2.1 TOP 10 TARGETED MARKETS IN THE PRESIDENTIAL RACE

MARKET	TOTAL SPOTS AIRED
Albuquerque-Santa Fe	9,758
Portland, Oregon	9,618
Philadelphia	9,021
Seattle-Tacoma	9,015
Detroit	8,938
Green Bay-Appleton	8,551
Grand Rapids	8,349
Kansas City	8,215
Milwaukee	8,139
St. Louis	7,963

Source: Based on data from Wisconsin Advertising Project.

TABLE 2.2   BUSH ADVANTAGE MARKETS

MARKET	BUSH ADVANTAGE (SPOTS)
San Diego	2,504
Jacksonville-Brunswick	2,475
Miami-Ft. Lauderdale	2,163
Sacramento-Stockton-Modesto	2,132
Mobile-Pensacola	1,905
Spokane	1,714
Fresno-Visalia	1,602
Los Angeles	1,447
Boston	1,247
Charleston-Huntington	1,216

Source: Based on data from Wisconsin Advertising Project.

the other hand, using simple proportions, a two-to-one advantage could be literally 2-to-1 or 1,000-to-500 or 5,000-to-2,500.

Accordingly, Figure 2.1 presents a market-by-market comparison of the two campaigns by plotting Gore ad totals versus Bush ad totals. A 50-50 line bisects the scatter plot. In markets on or near this line, the campaigns were evenly matched. Points above the line represent markets where Bush had an advantage and points below the line represent markets where Gore had an advantage. This sort of plot enables one to gauge both the absolute size of an advantage and whether that advantage was gained in a heavily or lightly targeted market.

TABLE 2.3   GORE ADVANTAGE MARKETS

MARKET	GORE ADVANTAGE (SPOTS)
Detroit	1,754
Philadelphia	1,747
St. Louis	1,670
Milwaukee	1,630
Albuquerque-Santa Fe	1,540
Green Bay-Appleton	1,129
Portland, Oregon	1,090
Flint-Saginaw-Bay City	962
Cleveland	834
Kansas City	743

Source: Based on data from Wisconsin Advertising Project.

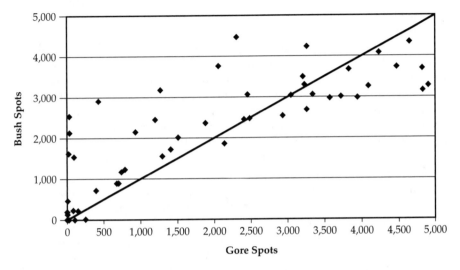

FIGURE 2.1 **BUSH VERSUS GORE BY MARKET**

Source: Based on data from Wisconsin Advertising Project.

Approximately two out of three markets (forty-eight out of seventy-five) had essentially the same level of advertising by each candidate. In markets with different levels of spots aired by the respective campaigns, the Gore forces had the advantage in eleven markets and Bush and his allies had the advantage in sixteen markets.

As Figure 2.1 illustrates, Bush generally had an advantage in markets that were targeted at lower levels, or in the case of the California markets (Fresno, Los Angeles, Sacramento, San Diego, and San Francisco), in areas that were not targeted at all by the Gore campaign. (These are the points in the upper-left-hand corner of the plot.) In hindsight, the money spent by the Republicans in California and the advantage that they built up was probably one of the biggest mistakes of this—and perhaps any—presidential campaign. Not only did Bush end up losing California decisively, but the advertising blitz aired on his behalf failed to bait the Gore campaign to invest significant Democratic resources in the state.

The Republicans, however, also enjoyed advantages in ads aired in more crucial markets and states. Most notably, the Bush campaign and its allies easily won the air war in Miami, Mobile (which covers the Florida panhandle), Charleston (West Virginia), and Boston (covering New Hampshire). Both Florida and New Hampshire were won by Bush by a handful of votes and West Virginia is typically a reliably Democratic state that Bush won in 2000. A Gore victory in any one of those three states would have given him the presidency.

As Figure 2.1 illustrates, the Gore advantage was generally in states that were being targeted at very high levels. (Those points in the upper-right-hand corner of the scatter plot). Specifically, the Democratic ticket had advantages in big markets in important swing states such as Michigan, Pennsylvania, Missouri, Wisconsin, Oregon, and Ohio. Still, even though Gore did have the advantage in crucial markets such as Detroit, Philadelphia, and St. Louis, these markets were not ignored by the Bush forces. Furthermore, it is important to note the generally cluttered advertising environment in those markets, which also had competitive Senate and House races. In fact, the markets where Gore had an advantage, were the most heavily targeted markets in the whole country for all political advertising.

The preceding analysis involved aggregating spots over the entire course of the campaign. But campaigns are dynamic and it is possible that unbalanced flows of advertising messages in particular markets at particular times were masked by aggregating the data to the entire campaign period. Figure 2.2 shows national totals for advertising by week over the course of the campaign. It shows that the advertising campaign began early in the summer and that the volume of campaign advertising in the presidential race increased dramatically as Election Day neared. It also shows advantages for Gore in August and advantages for Bush in the last two weeks of the campaign. How did these national trends in the timing of the air war translate at the market level?

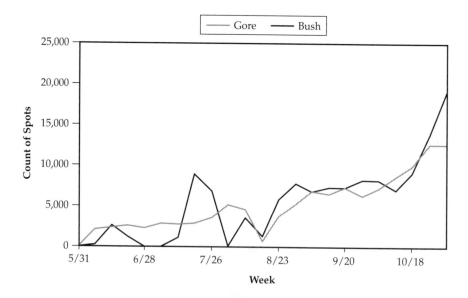

FIGURE 2.2 BUSH VERSUS GORE OVER TIME

Source: Based on data from Wisconsin Advertising Project.

TABLE 2.4 **MARKET ADVANTAGES IN PRESIDENTIAL RACE FOR AUGUST**

		GORE ADS			
		MINIMAL (0–50)	*LOW* (51–321)	*MEDIUM* (322–591)	*HIGH* (592+)
BUSH ADS	*Minimal*	36 markets with no advertising	Washington, D.C. Spokane		
	Low	Miami Las Vegas Raleigh Greensboro Mobile Rochester	Charleston Dayton	Lexington Des Moines New Orleans Little Rock Portland, ME Louisville Orlando	Albuquerque
	Medium		Atlanta	Chicago Cincinnati Kansas City Harrisburg Wilkes Barre West Palm Beach Tampa Toledo Columbus	Flint St. Louis Portland, OR Milwaukee Detroit Cleveland Pittsburgh Grand Rapids Green Bay Philadelphia Seattle
	High				

Source: Based on data from Wisconsin Advertising Project.

Table 2.4 illustrates the competitive picture in August 2000—just as the ad war was heating up, but before saturation levels hit many markets. It shows that the Gore campaign enjoyed spot advantages in twenty-one key markets (places like Albuquerque, Detroit, Green Bay, Milwaukee, and Pittsburgh) and faced a small deficit in only one key market (Miami). Although Gore's lead by the end of August was obviously due to many factors perhaps some of the Gore bounce was due to the advantage he enjoyed in paid media in key markets.

Bush's massive advertising advantage in the last two weeks did not really translate into advantages at the market level. Although there were more markets below the diagonal in Table 2.5 (page 34), which show places where Bush had an advantage, most of these markets were in California. During the last two weeks, the one market in a swing state where Bush had a significant advantage in the flow of advertising was Jacksonville, Florida. The Republican ticket had smaller advantages in the Mobile-Pensacola market (covering the Florida panhandle), Boston, Portland, Maine, and Chicago. Again, it

TABLE 2.5 MARKET ADVANTAGES IN PRESIDENTIAL RACE FOR LAST TWO WEEKS

		GORE ADS			
		MINIMAL (0–200)	LOW (201–500)	MEDIUM (501–799)	HIGH (800+)
BUSH ADS	Minimal	Albany Atlanta Austin Baltimore Birmingham Buffalo Charlotte Dallas Denver Greensboro Greenville Hartford San Antonio Houston Indianapolis Lexington Louisville Rochester New Orleans New York Norfolk Okl. City Phoenix Providence Raleigh Richmond Roanoke Salt Lake City Wichita Syracuse Tulsa Washington			
	Low	Toledo Omaha San Francisco Fresno	Cleveland Columbus Dayton Cincinnati		
	Medium	Sacramento	Mobile Boston Portland, ME Chicago	Wilkes Barre Memphis Flint Nashville West Palm Beach Charleston	
	High	Los Angeles San Diego	Jacksonville	Harrisburg Knoxville Little Rock Miami Philadelphia Seattle Spokane	Albuquerque Green Bay Milwaukee Portland, OR Detroit Orlando Des Moines Kansas City St. Louis Las Vegas Gr. Rapids Tampa

Source: Based on data from Wisconsin Advertising Project.

is important to note that these modest Bush advantages could have been more pronounced if not for the decision to invest so heavily in California.

Campaign strategists are of two different minds about early versus late advertising. On the one hand, some argue that an early advertising blitz is not as likely to get lost in the clutter of the last weeks of the campaign and may be more likely to catch people when they are still persuadable. Other strategists believe that a late blitz keeps campaign messages fresh in voters' minds as they enter the polling booths and may capture swing voters just when they are paying attention to the campaign. Although not tackled in this chapter, these questions are of course empirical ones that are not only of interest to social scientists but to campaign strategists as well. In future work, the dynamic and comprehensive nature of the CMAG data can help us answer them.

FIVE CASES

In this second part, I examine in more detail the nature of the 2000 presidential election air war in five markets. Each of the markets (Pittsburgh, Detroit, Miami, Little Rock, and Nashville) was located in an important state decided by fewer than four percentage points. Were the campaigns evenly matched in these battleground markets? At the risk of giving away the punch line, this analysis will show that even strategically important markets in crucial states had different patterns of television advertising and, more importantly, had unbalanced flows of advertising messages during key parts of the campaign.

Figure 2.3 (page 36) shows the air war in Pittsburgh over the course of the campaign. The Gore campaign was on the air first and was more active during most of June and July airing around 100 spots per week during this early summer time period. The Bush campaign made a heavy buy in late July (almost 300 spots in one week) and then went dark for a couple weeks in August while the Gore forces aired almost 200 spots a week in the time period around the Democratic convention. From Labor Day on, the two sides were evenly matched in their buys, with the volume rising to 400 spots per side in the last weeks of the campaign. In mid-October, the Democrats had an advantage as they aired about 100 more ads per week than the Republicans. The Democratic ticket ended up enjoying a modest advantage in advertising in the Pittsburgh market with most of that advantage being built up in August and the remainder in the last two weeks of the contest.

The air war in Detroit is illustrated in Figure 2.4 (page 37). Both sides were engaged from early summer, but the Gore campaign was always engaged at a higher level. This generally higher level of activity along with more significant advantages built up in August and early October resulted

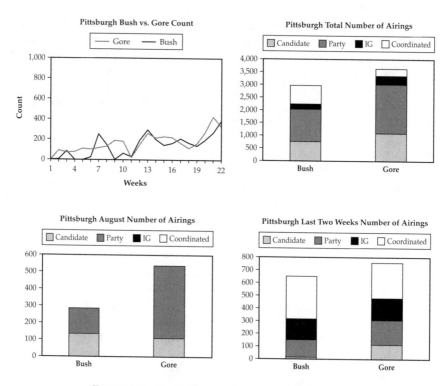

FIGURE 2.3   PITTSBURGH BALANCE OF ADVERTISING

Source: Based on data from Wisconsin Advertising Project.

in the Democratic forces enjoying a 1,700 spot advantage by the end of the campaign. Although it did not translate into such a hefty advantage in most other markets, the pattern in the Bush advertising is one that was apparent in a number of other places—modest buys over the summer in comparison to Gore and very heavy buys at the end, which somewhat made up for a campaign-long deficit. A similar picture emerged in Flint, while the two sides were more equal in Grand Rapids.

Advertising activity in Miami is portrayed in Figure 2.5 (page 38). The Bush campaign made a very heavy buy in late July and early August, went dark for a couple weeks, and then steadily raised their advertising buys in the biggest Florida market. During the last week of the election, the Bush campaign and their allies aired close to 600 spots. More importantly, the Bush forces had Miami to themselves for most of the campaign. The Democratic ticket did not make any buys until after Labor Day and only in early October did they begin to match Republican buys. Furthermore, they did not match the big GOP buys in the last two weeks of the campaign. When all

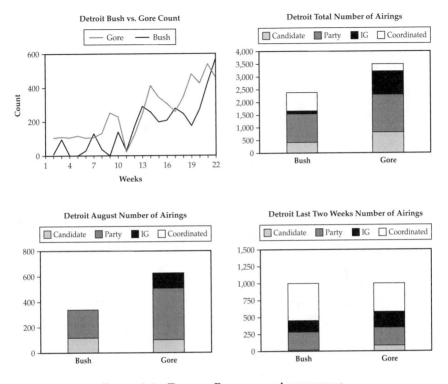

FIGURE 2.4   DETROIT BALANCE OF ADVERTISING

Source: Based on data from Wisconsin Advertising Project.

was aired in Miami, the Bush forces had put more than twice as many spots on the air in Miami (more than 2,000 spots) than the Gore forces. With lower levels of ads, the competitive picture was the same in two other Florida markets (Jacksonville and Mobile-Pensacola). The two sides were evenly matched in the Orlando and West Palm Beach markets and the Bush forces had a modest advantage in Tampa. Although my goal in this chapter is not to make causal claims, it is certainly noteworthy that in a state decided by a mere 500 votes, the Republicans had significant advantages in three of the six major media markets.

Advertising flows in Little Rock ended up being even (see Figure 2.6 on page 39). Nevertheless, there were differences in how the two sides got to their 3,000 spots each in Arkansas's capital city. The Gore forces built a modest advantage with modest buys over the summer. Both forces were evenly matched—albeit at levels lower than most other competitive markets. (Total advertising activity in Little Rock in the presidential race was about two-thirds that of advertising activity in Detroit.) The Bush forces, however, made a very

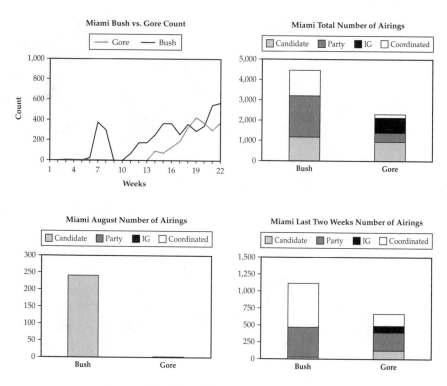

FIGURE 2.5   MIAMI BALANCE OF ADVERTISING

Source: Based on data from Wisconsin Advertising Project.

heavy buy in the last week. This buy (over 600 spots) was one of their biggest in the country and gave them a significant advantage in the Little Rock market during the last two weeks of the campaign.

Nashville, the biggest market in Al Gore's home state and the site of his national campaign headquarters, was quiet for most of the campaign (see Figure 2.7 on page 40). The first buys were made in early October and the only buys of any real significance were made in the final week of the campaign. In the week before the election, the Republicans had 400 spots up on the air. When all was said and aired, the GOP ticket had a 200 spot advantage in this late-targeted market. The picture was identical in Memphis and Knoxville.

CONCLUSION

Whether and how elite-generated information influences ordinary citizens' political judgments has been an enduring question in social science research. In this chapter, I took advantage of a new technology to describe the timing

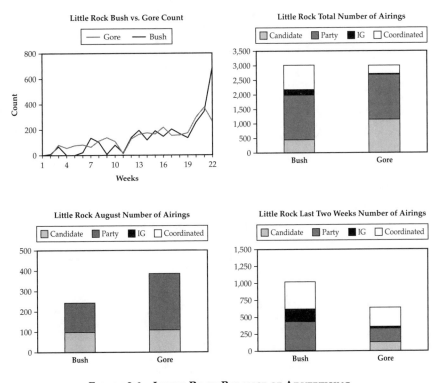

FIGURE 2.6   LITTLE ROCK BALANCE OF ADVERTISING

Source: Based on data from Wisconsin Advertising Project.

and geographic targeting of advertisements in the 2000 presidential campaign. I was not testing a specific theory, nor did I attempt to model or draw any conclusions about the effect of these commercials on voting behavior, turnout, or campaign issue knowledge. My more modest objective was to learn from the data and sketch out what will be an important source of information for future studies of advertising influence and campaign strategies.

The targeting data presented in this chapter teach us a number of important lessons about how to study advertising in presidential elections. One, the presidential campaign air war did not start at the national conventions or Labor Day, but much earlier in the summer. Accordingly, studies of presidential campaigns must start early in the summer. Two, party and interest groups were important players in the air war and must be included in any sort of analysis of advertising in presidential elections. Three, the advertising air war took place on local television and scholars must search for advertising effects at the market level. Studies or measures of campaign advertising that use national measures of presidential campaigns and presidential advertising lose considerable information.

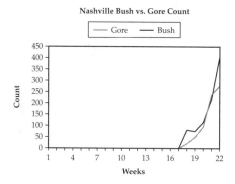

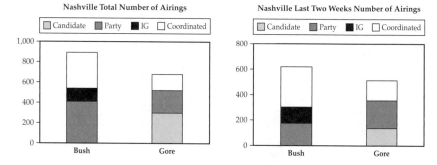

FIGURE 2.7   NASHVILLE BALANCE OF ADVERTISING

Source: Based on data from Wisconsin Advertising Project.

I hope that this chapter provides important substantive information for scholars hoping to better understand the effect of advertising in presidential elections. Although the two tickets and their party allies and interest group allies were evenly matched nationally, there was significant heterogeneity in the volume of the advertising from market to market. Even very important markets were targeted for different levels of campaign advertising. In some strategically crucial markets there were also unbalanced flows of information. For example, the Gore forces had a significant advantage in Detroit and the Bush forces had a significant advantage in Miami. Furthermore, even in markets that ended up being even, there were unbalanced flows at particular points during the campaign. In general, the Democrats had advantages in a number of key markets in August while the Republicans launched a big advertising push in the last week of the campaign. Finally, there were differences in when markets were engaged. Residents of the Detroit and Pittsburgh media markets began seeing advertising early in the summer, residents of Miami had to wait until late summer, and Volunteer State citizens in Knoxville, Memphis, and Nashville were only exposed to the air war at the very end of the campaign. Of course, many markets saw no advertising at all.

What do these findings mean? Typically, presidential campaigns are considered to be poor places to look for campaign effects in general and advertising effects in particular. Given theoretical expectations about the effect of unbalanced flows of information, the geographic and temporal differences in targeting that were described earlier create the variance in advertising exposure that is necessary to measure advertising effects. The temporal and cross-sectional variance documented in the 2000 campaign creates conditions under which we would expect to find effects at the individual level. Even in an evenly matched race with a strong focus on particular strategically important markets, there was actually great variance and significant heterogeneity in the volume and balance of advertising from market to market and from time period to time period. In short, although detailed survey and vote data will be needed to tease out the effects, there is substantial variance in the political contexts where voters reside.

Even—or perhaps especially—in a year like 2000, previous voting patterns and fundamental attitudes and attachments surely had a much greater influence on the vote choice than did TV advertising. This argument would come as no surprise to political practitioners. Candidates and their advisors know that ad campaigns do not win the presidency by themselves and that they must play with the cards they are dealt—past voting patterns, the partisan composition of the electorate, the state of the economy, and America's place in the world. Television advertising may matter at the margin—where a few percentage points can be decisive. This chapter looked for places and times where that marginal effect was most likely to occur.

REFERENCES

Finkel, Steven. "Re-examining the Minimal Effects Model in Recent Presidential Campaigns." *Journal of Politics* 55 (1993): 1–21.

Goldstein, Ken, and Paul Freedman. "Lessons Learned: Campaign Advertising in the 2000 Elections." *Political Communication* 19, no. 1 (2002).

Goldstein, Ken, and Paul Freedman. "New Evidence for New Arguments: Money and Advertising in the 1996 Senate Elections." *Journal of Politics* 62, no. 4 (2000): 1087–1109.

Shaw, Darron. "The Effect of TV Ads and Candidate Appearances on Statewide Presidential Votes, 1988–1996." *American Political Science Review* 93 (2 June 1999): 345–361.

Zaller, John. *The Nature and Origins of Mass Opinion.* Cambridge: Cambridge University Press, 1992.

Zaller, John. "The Myth of Massive Media Impact Revisited." In *Political Persuasion and Attitude Change.* Ed. Diana Mutz, Paul Sniderman, and Richard Brody. Ann Arbor: University of Michigan Press, 1996.

NOTES

1. Support for the purchase and analysis of the data used in this paper was provided by The Pew Charitable Trusts. I would like to thank Mike Franz, Travis Ridout, and Joel Rivlin for their research assistance. Portions of the analysis in this chapter were first reported in Goldstein and Freedman (2002).
2. Market totals by candidate and tone for 1996 are available at <http://www.polisci.wisc.edu/tvadvertising>.

Television Advertising
in the 2000 Congressional Elections

Paul S. Herrnson

The advent of a new form of campaigning by political parties and interest groups, often referred to as "issue advocacy" advertising, has had a major impact on the roles of these organizations in congressional elections. These organizations have supplemented their traditional efforts in candidate recruitment, political agenda setting, the provision of campaign contributions and services, and voter mobilization with television campaign advertisements that are designed to have a direct impact on the outcomes of individual elections. During the 2000 elections, parties and interest groups spent a record sum of more than $115 million on televised advertising intended to affect the outcomes of House and Senate elections, most of it on issue advocacy.[1] Issue advocacy advertising changed the dynamics of many close congressional elections, increasing their costs and reducing the candidates' ability to set the campaign agenda or control the messages communicated to voters.

Party and interest group television ads and increased activity in other areas of campaigning, such as direct-mail advertising and fundraising, are part of a larger trend that began in the latter part of the twentieth century. During the middle part of that century, congressional elections were largely candidate-centered. Most candidates were self-recruited, assembled their own organizations and financial resources, assumed responsibility for most aspects of their own campaigns, and competed with their opponent in a battle over votes that involved campaign communications and voter mobilization.[2] During the late 1970s and early 1980s, national party organizations began to play supplemental roles in selected House and Senate campaigns, providing candidates with assistance in a variety of activities requiring technical expertise, in-depth research, or connections with political consultants, interest groups, and others who possessed some of the resources needed to wage a competitive campaign. A small group of PACs began to provide similar forms of assistance. Nevertheless, congressional campaigns remained candidate-centered.[3] With few exceptions, the candidates were firmly in control of the campaign messages disseminated to voters.

This chapter analyzes political party and interest group strategies and television advertising in the 2000 congressional elections to determine how issue advocacy electioneering has challenged conventional wisdom on the nature of candidate-centered campaigns. Using data collected by the Campaign Media Analysis Group (CMAG), I assess the timing, distribution, focus, and tone of the television advertisements broadcast by political parties and interest groups. I demonstrate that issue advocacy advertising has enabled parties and interest groups to play a more significant role in congressional elections.

ELECTION STRATEGIES OF POLITICAL PARTIES AND INTEREST GROUPS

Political parties in the United States are first and foremost concerned with electing candidates to public office. Because American politicians and parties are more pragmatic than they are ideological, winning control of the government takes precedence over enacting specific policies or promoting an overall vision for society. Party leaders recognize that their ability to enact change or preserve the status quo depends on electing individual politicians to exercise control over the levers of government. Candidates and party leaders make strategic adjustments in issue stances, rhetoric, and relationships with voters and other groups in order to improve their prospects of winning or maintaining power. Candidates, party committees, and interest groups adapt to the changing organizational and resource demands associated with campaigning.

Beginning in the late 1970s, first the Republicans and then the Democrats began to strengthen their party organizations at the national level. At this time, the Democratic and Republican National Committees, and the Democratic Congressional Campaign Committee (DCCC), the Democratic Senatorial Campaign Committee (DSCC), the National Republican Congressional Committee (NRCC), and the National Republican Senatorial Committee (NRSC) became organizationally stable, fiscally solvent, hired staffs with specialized campaign skills, and adopted professional-bureaucratic decision-making procedures. These "institutionalized" national party committees amassed the wherewithal to play a significant role in federal elections, eclipsing the influence of state and local party committees in those contests.[4]

The congressional and senatorial campaign committees (sometimes referred to as the "Hill committees" because they were originally located in congressional office space) formulate most party strategy in House and Senate elections. These groups have one overall goal: to maximize the number of seats their party controls in Congress. They concentrate the vast majority of their efforts on the election contests they anticipate will be competitive. Ideology, policy positions, race, ethnicity, gender, and other idiosyncrasies associated with individual candidates and campaigns are considered only if they have the potential to affect the competitiveness of an election.[5] As Senator Mitch McConnell, NRSC chair during the 1998 and 2000 elections, explained:

> In doing my job as the chairman of the senatorial committee, the only criteria is, How close are you? I can't joust with windmills; and I'm not going to fund landslides. And we make the decision every day by the numbers. I get tracking polls from the states where we're competitive across the country. I have no particular bias in favor of or against any of our candidates. The only issue is, How close are you?[6]

National conditions influence party leaders' assessments of which seats are likely to be hotly contested. The partisan distribution of seats in Congress, presidential popularity, the strength of the economy, and the public's level of satisfaction with the performance of the government and the state of the nation can have an impact on how a party distributes its campaign resources. Public satisfaction with the status quo typically encourages the Hill committees of the president's party to employ an "offensive" strategy that commits more campaign resources to challenger and open-seat candidates' campaigns. Popular dissatisfaction encourages those committees to employ a "defensive" strategy that distributes more resources to endangered incumbents. The out-party has the opposite response to national conditions. When national conditions favor the president's party, the out-party typically uses a "defensive" strategy; when conditions are to the disadvantage of the president's party, the out-party uses an "offensive" one.[7]

Many of the national conditions surrounding the 2000 congressional elections suggested that the Democrats were likely to employ an offensive strategy and the Republicans would use a defensive strategy. The Republicans held majorities—albeit relatively slim ones—in the House and Senate, the economy was strong, and the public was fairly satisfied with the government's performance and the state of the nation. President Clinton also enjoyed relatively high approval ratings for his job performance. These factors suggested that the Democrats would invest more resources in the campaigns of challengers and open-seat contestants. However, presidential approval numbers told only part of the story because a large portion of the electorate disapproved of the president's personal conduct. Similarly, the presidential election was extremely close throughout the campaign season. A final variable that influenced party decision making was that relatively few seats were considered competitive.[8] This enabled party decision makers, particularly the congressional campaign committees, to pay less attention to national conditions than usual in favor of devoting more time to assessing the nuances of individual elections. Overall, the environment leading up to the election encouraged the Democratic Hill committees to employ a moderate offensive strategy that delivered most but not all of their resources to Democratic challengers and open-seat candidates. These conditions led the Republicans to employ a moderate defensive strategy that focused considerable resources on GOP incumbents' campaigns.

Interest groups have a broader set of goals and employ a more diverse set of strategies than do parties. Groups that consider elections to be their most important means for influencing the policy process use what are usually referred to as "ideological" strategies.[9] Because these groups' major goal is to maximize the number of members of Congress who share their issue positions or overall political perspective, they distribute most of their election resources in ways that are designed to help sympathetic candidates involved in close races. Ideological groups are similar to party committees in this regard. However, they are more likely to become involved in congressional primaries than are party organizations, which often do not participate in congressional elections until after a candidate has won the nomination.

Groups that view the distribution of campaign resources as a way to make their direct legislative lobbying easier employ what are called "access" strategies.[10] They support incumbents of both parties, using most of their resources to advance the candidacies of party leaders, committee chairs, and other incumbents who are in a position to influence legislation that ranks high on the group's priority list. These groups typically ignore challengers who are sympathetic to their views because most challengers have poor electoral prospects. Of course, the group's decision to ignore challengers typically seals these candidates' fate. However, access-oriented groups will support open-seat candidates who share the group's views and have reasonable chances of winning. The campaign spending patterns of access-oriented groups are influenced less by the conditions present in a particular election season than are those of ideological groups.

Many groups, including most labor unions, employ what are usually labeled "mixed" strategies because they combine both ideological and access strategies. Like ideological groups, they distribute some election resources to help candidates who share the groups' views and are involved competitive contests. Like access-oriented groups, they distribute some resources in ways that are designed to ingratiate the group with incumbents who are in positions to affect the group's policy priorities.

Party organizations and interest groups participate in congressional elections in a variety of ways: They recruit candidates to run for the House and Senate; they provide selected candidates with cash contributions; and they provide assistance in campaign management, strategic research, communications, and other aspects of campaigning requiring technical expertise, and in-depth research.[11] They also help candidates collect the money and other resources needed to mount a viable campaign from prospective donors and consultants. Much of this assistance, which is directly coordinated with a candidate's campaign, is regulated by the Federal Election Campaign Act (FECA). Most party assistance of this type is financed with "hard money," which is raised and spent within the confines of the FECA. Similarly, most interest group assistance is provided by political action committees (PACs), which are subject to the FECA's contribution, spending, and reporting requirements. Party and PAC independent expenditures, which can only be made without the knowledge or consent of a federal candidate, also are subject to the FECA's regulations. These have been reviewed in detail elsewhere.[12]

Political parties and interest groups also conduct campaign activities that are not fully regulated by the FECA. Parties and groups seek to set a national political agenda that works to the advantage of their candidates.[13] Democrats and their interest group allies work to encourage voters to focus on Social Security, health care reform, environmental protections, or education when casting their ballots. These policy concerns are traditionally favorably associated with the Democratic Party, and its candidates benefit when these issues comprise the basis for citizens' voting decisions. Republicans and their allies endeavor to set a political agenda based on tax cuts, crime and drug abuse prevention, cutting government waste, and family values—voting issues that traditionally help GOP candidates. Some of these efforts are financed with hard money, but a significant portion is financed with "soft money," which is raised and spent outside of the FECA's regulatory regime.

The collapse of the FECA has enabled parties and groups to spend both hard and soft money on other election activities. Such funds are used to register and mobilize voters who are sympathetic to the organizations' preferred candidates and to broadcast so-called issue advocacy ads. These ads are similar to candidate ads in most respects, except they tend to be more negative and are not supposed to be coordinated with candidate campaigns.[14] The legal distinction between candidate and issue ads rests on two qualifications: First, issue ads do not qualify for the discounted preemptive airtime to which candidates are entitled, and second, issue ads are prohibited from *expressly* advocating the election or defeat of a specific candidate. Nevertheless, these legal differences are of little substantive consequence because most candidates purchase nonpreemptive airtime to ensure their ads are broadcast during popular viewing times, and few candidate ads expressly ask voters to elect or vote for themselves or defeat or vote against their opponents.[15]

DATA AND METHODS

Television advertising has played a prominent role in most congressional elections for several decades. The CMAG data, which record the date, time, and content of every television ad aired in connection with congressional elections in the nation's seventy-five largest media markets, make it possible to learn about campaign advertising practices in 402 of the House contests and 33 of the Senate races in 2000.[16] It is important to note that not all of the campaigns in constituencies covered by these media markets advertised on television. The high costs of TV advertising, an imperfect match between the borders of many congressional districts and media markets, and a lack of competition discouraged many House candidates from advertising on broadcast television. House campaigns broadcast ads in 161 of the districts covered by the largest seventy-five media markets, and Senate campaigns aired ads in twenty-nine of the states covered by them. These figures do not include ads disseminated via cable television, which are excluded from the analysis.

The ads included in the CMAG data were coded according to their sponsor (candidate, party, or interest group), whether they occurred during a primary or general election, the week they were aired, their substantive focus (candidate performance or substantive issues), and tone (positive, negative, or contrast). The party, incumbency, and competitiveness of the candidate also were recorded to make generalizations about the distribution of party and interest group ads possible. (For more information about the coding of the data see the Appendix). The data were analyzed using descriptive statistics that report the frequency of ads broadcast by different groups of sponsors in a variety of races. The ad frequencies are an excellent measure of parties' and groups' communications efforts because they record the actual number of spots citizens had the opportunity to view rather than estimate party and group expenditures, which are affected by local costs.[17] Costs vary across the election season, in part, because station owners' raise them in responses to politicians' and other customers' demands. The discussions of the ad frequencies refer to the total number of ads of any type broadcast, not the number of unique ads aired. In other words, if three unique ads were each aired five times, they would be counted as a total of fifteen—not three—ads.

TELEVISED ISSUE ADVOCACY
OF POLITICAL PARTIES AND INTEREST GROUPS

Television advertising has been widely used by congressional candidates in recent years. Roughly 70 percent of all major-party House candidates competing in the 1998 general elections aired TV ads. These accounted for 17 percent of the typical House candidate's campaign expenditures, making it the largest item in their campaign budgets. Nine of ten Senate campaigns broadcast TV ads during that same year. These accounted for 30 percent of the typical Senate candidate's campaign spending.[18]

Political parties first took to the airwaves in connection with congressional elections in 1980, when the Republican National Committee (RNC) aired generic party-focused television ads stating: "Vote Republican. For a

Change." Both parties aired a few generic issue ads in 1982 and some subsequent elections.[19] Interest groups made their presence felt on TV in the 1980 elections, when the National Conservative Political Action Committee (NCPAC) ran independent expenditure ads attacking several Democrat House members and six Democratic senators for voting to approve the Panama Canal Treaty. Four of the six senators lost, and NCPAC claimed credit for their defeat.[20]

Federal Election Commission rulings and court decisions handed down in response to the efforts of politicians, party organizations, and interest groups weakened the FECA over the course of the 1980s and 1990s, creating new revenue sources and spending avenues for parties and groups. As a result of these decisions, both sets of organizations felt empowered to broadcast substantial numbers of candidate-focused issue advocacy ads during the 1996 elections.[21] These ads became a prominent feature in most competitive congressional elections during the 1998 campaign season, in some cases drowning out the campaign communications disseminated by the candidates.[22] Issue advocacy electioneering reached record proportions in the 2000 contests.

Political parties and interest groups televise issue ads in congressional elections to accomplish several objectives. First, they use them to influence the campaign agenda. As noted earlier, parties air some ads to set a national political agenda that is favorable to their candidates. Party committees and some interest groups also broadcast ads for the purpose of setting the campaign agenda in individual House and Senate contests. Second, political parties and interest groups broadcast issue advocacy spots to reinforce a campaign's message, either by focusing on the candidate's job performance or issue positions. Third, parties and interest groups have increasingly used issue ads to attack an opponent's job performance, issue positions, or character. These ads, some of which are purely negative and others of which contrast the candidates, are used to create doubts in the minds of swing voters, mobilize a candidate's supporters, or demobilize an opponent's base. Parties and groups also air these ads for the purpose of forcing an opponent to divert scarce resources from communicating his or her core message to fending off the attack. Depriving an opponent of airtime is a fourth objective parties and groups seek to accomplish when purchasing issue ads late in the campaign.[23]

Party and interest group advertising occupied a substantial portion of the television airwaves during the 2000 election season. Candidates, who are the prime actors in the U.S. candidate-centered election system, aired 61 percent of the 145,458 TV ads aired in connection with House elections. Parties and interest groups accounted for 22 percent and 17 percent, respectively (see Table 3.1 on page 50). Democratic candidates and party organizations aired slightly more ads than did their Republican counterparts. The number of party sponsored and interest group–sponsored ads

TABLE 3.1   THE SPONSORS OF TELEVISION
ADVERTISEMENTS IN THE 2000 CONGRESSIONAL ELECTIONS

	HOUSE	SENATE
Democratic candidates	31%	38%
Republican candidates	30	34
Democratic Party	12	13
Republican Party	10	10
Interest groups	17	5
Total ads	237,088	236,807

Note: Table includes only major-party candidates. (It excludes a small number of ads on behalf minor-party and independent candidates.) The figure for Republicans includes 148 ads that New York's Conservative party aired on behalf of Rick Lazio.

Source: Compiled from data provided by the Wisconsin Advertising Project.

that flashed across television screens in connection with the 2000 House elections would have been unimaginable fifteen years ago when virtually all of the ads aired in connection with congressional races originated with the candidate.

A small number of organizations accounted for most of the interest group advertising in House races. Citizens for a Better Medicare, representing the interests of the pharmaceutical industry, along with the American Federation of Labor-Congress of Industrial Organizations (AFL-CIO) were the sources of most of the interest group ads in races for the lower chamber. To illustrate, the AFL-CIO alone accounted for 28 percent of all interest group ads (see Table 3.2). Just four groups, including three associated with conservative causes, accounted for 78 percent of the ads. Groups

TABLE 3.2   THE TOP INTEREST GROUP SPONSORS OF TELEVISION
POLITICAL ADVERTISEMENTS IN THE 2000 CONGRESSIONAL ELECTIONS

HOUSE		SENATE	
AFL-CIO	28%	Chamber of Commerce	15%
Citizens for Better Medicare	27	Americans for Quality Nursing Home Care	12
Chamber of Commerce	14	Americans for Job Security	12
Business Round Table	9	League of Conservation Voters	11
U.S. Term Limits	2	Business Roundtable	9
Twenty-three other groups	20	Twenty-two other groups	41
Total ads	40,450	Total ads	12,980

Note: Includes only major-party candidates.

Source: Compiled from data provided by the Wisconsin Advertising Project.

TABLE 3.3 THE SPONSORS OF INTEREST GROUP TELEVISION
ADVERTISEMENTS IN THE 2000 CONGRESSIONAL ELECTIONS

	HOUSE	SENATE
Businesses	52%	52%
Labor unions	31	4
Ideological groups	14	35
Party leadership groups	1	8
Unknown	2	—
Total ads	40,450	12,980

Notes: "—" = less than 0.5%. Some columns may not add to 100 percent due to rounding. Includes only major-party candidates.
Source: Compiled from data provided by the Wisconsin Advertising Project.

representing business interests (including trade associations) were the most highly represented of all the different types of interest organizations that broadcast ads in the 2000 House races, accounting for over half of them, whereas labor was responsible for just under one-third (see Table 3.3). Ideological groups, led by U.S. Term Limits, Americans for Limited Terms (ALT), and Campaign for a Progressive Future, championing gun control, broadcast 14 percent of the ads. Organizations affiliated with party leaders produced a mere 1 percent. Among all interest groups, economic interests clearly had the upper hand in House races.

The rise of issue advocacy has had a similar, but perhaps slightly less pronounced, effect on Senate elections. Candidates aired 72 percent of all of the television ads broadcast in connection with the 2000 Senate elections. Parties and interest groups accounted for 23 percent and 5 percent, respectively. Despite the fact that House candidates greatly outnumbered Senate candidates, the number of total ads aired in connection with each chamber was almost identical. Party committees accounted for similar levels of activity in Senate campaigns as in House campaigns, but interest groups aired substantially more ads in the battle for control of the House. Democratic candidates and party committees broadcast more TV ads than did GOP candidates and parties in races for the Senate. Representatives of organized business broadcast over half of all interest group ads in both Senate and House races. In contrast to elections for the House, workers were barely heard among the din of pro-business ads in contests for the Senate, where labor accounted for a mere 4 percent of the total interest group ads broadcast. Ideological groups and organizations affiliated with party leaders were much more active in Senate contests than in the House. The number of groups broadcasting significant numbers of TV ads in conjunction with the race for control over the Senate was larger than in the contest for majority control of the House. Indeed, the top five groups broadcast ads in the 2000 Senate races for only 59 percent of the total.

TABLE 3.4   THE DISTRIBUTION OF PARTY TELEVISION
ADVERTISEMENTS IN THE 2000 CONGRESSIONAL ELECTIONS

	HOUSE		SENATE	
	DEMOCRATS	REPUBLICANS	DEMOCRATS	REPUBLICANS
Incumbent				
Very competitive	12%	19%	22%	39%
Moderately competitive	2	14	1	2
Uncompetitive	1	—	—	—
Challenger				
Very competitive	29%	16%	28%	24%
Moderately competitive	18	4	2	1
Uncompetitive	—	—	1	1
Open-Seat				
Very competitive	21%	28%	24%	30%
Moderately competitive	16	19	21	4
Uncompetitive	—	—	—	—
Total ads	28,930	23,917	30,610	22,412

Notes: A very competitive race is defined as a contest decided by 10 points or less; a moderately competitive race is defined as a contest decided by 11–20 points; and an uncompetitive race is defined as a contest decided by 21 points or more. Some columns may not add to 100 percent due to rounding. "—" = less than 0.5%. Includes only major-party candidates. The figure for Republicans includes 137 ads that New York's Conservative party aired on behalf of Ric Lazio.

Source: Compiled from data provided by the Wisconsin Advertising Project.

THE DISTRIBUTION OF PARTY AND INTEREST GROUP ADS

Parties broadcast the vast majority of their issue advocacy ads in close contests, as would be expected given their seat maximization goals (see Table 3.4). This pattern bears some similarity to that typically reported for campaign contributions and coordinated expenditures, but the ads are concentrated on a smaller set of races.[24] Both parties did a good job allocating their communications resources to close House races. Each aired roughly 63 percent of its ads in very competitive races—those decided by 10 percent or less of the two-party vote. The parties aired all but 1 percent of the remainder of their spots in moderately close contests, wasting virtually no funds on campaigns that were not considered competitive during at least one point in the campaign. Democratic party committees broadcast almost one-half of their ads to help their party's challengers and only 15 percent to aid its incumbents, reflecting their moderate offensive strategy. Republican party organizations, by contrast, broadcast only one-fifth of their ads to aid GOP challengers, and over one-third of their ads to aid the party's incumbents, reflecting their moderate defensive approach. The Republicans spent more of their communications resources on House open-seats than did the Democrats, but both parties committed substantial resources to them.

The open-seat race between Democrat Linda Chapin and Republican Richard Keller in the Florida's 8th district was the scene of some of the heaviest party issue advocacy campaigning. The seat was vacated when Republican Representative Bill McCollum decided to run for the Senate. Chapin had previously served as chair of the Orange County Commission, whereas Keller, an attorney, had no prior political experience. As is usually the case in close open-seat races, both candidates engaged in heavy spending: Chapin spent $1.7 million to Keller's $1.3 million.[25] Both parties also invested heavily. Democratic party committees broadcast 1,250 ads on Chapin's behalf. Most of these focused on education. The GOP ran 1,380 ads, focusing mainly on taxes, to help Keller. Keller ultimately won the hard-fought campaign with 51 percent of the vote to Chapin's 49 percent.

It is easier for parties to target their resources in Senate elections because party officials have to assess their candidates' prospects in only thirty-three or thirty-four races. Both parties targeted the vast majority of their issue advocacy ads in close contests, but the Republicans were more effective in this regard. GOP committees broadcast 93 percent of their TV spots in Senate races in very competitive contests, as opposed to the Democratic party committees, which broadcast 74 percent in those same contests. Neither party devoted significant resources to airing spots in seats that were not considered at least moderately competitive at one point in time. The distribution of party ads in Senate elections, like that in House contests, reflects the parties' overall 2000 campaign strategies. The Democrats were more aggressive than the Republicans, airing 31 percent of their ads to help Democratic challengers and only 23 percent to aid their incumbents. The Republicans broadcast only 26 percent of their ads in races with Republican challengers and another 41 percent in races with GOP incumbents. Both parties committed significant resources to Senate open-seat contests, but Democratic party committees aired considerably more spots in them than did their Republican rivals.

The election between Democratic Senator Chuck Robb and Republican challenger Governor George Allen in Virginia was the scene of the heaviest party issue advocacy spending in a Senate race. Robb was first elected to the Senate in 1988, after serving as Virginia's lieutenant governor and governor. But he was also very vulnerable. Several personal scandals and lack of visibility around the state almost cost Robb his seat to Republican Iran Contra figure and former Lieutenant Colonel Oliver North in 1994. Like Robb, Allen had a wealth of political experience, having served in the Virginia House of Delegates during the 1980s, in the U.S. House in the early 1990s, and as Virginia's governor between 1993 and 1997. While serving as governor, Allen enjoyed approval ratings as high as 68 percent. His prowess as a fundraiser and well-honed communications skills combined with Robb's political vulnerabilities to make the Virginia Senate one of the most closely watched races in 2000. Allen outspent Robb $10 million to $6.6 million.[26] Both parties became heavily involved. The Democratic Party spent more than $5 million and ran more than 6,700 television spots on behalf of Robb. The ads focused on issues such as education, health care, and abortion. The Republican Party was also very active, spending nearly $4 million for more than 5,300 spots that criticized Robb's record and championed Allen's position on tax cuts. In the end, Allen emerged the victor, winning with 52 percent of the vote to Robb's 48 percent.

Interest groups targeted their TV ads in some predictable and some not so predictable ways. As was the case with party committees, groups concentrated their ads on a small number of very competitive races. Like the parties, interest groups typically distribute their campaign contributions to a somewhat larger group.[27]

Business interests traditionally pursue fairly bipartisan access-oriented strategies when distributing campaign money, but they employed mixed strategies when airing issue ads in 2000.[28] Virtually all of the ads were broadcast to help Republicans, and most were used to help GOP incumbents (see Table 3.5). The National Association of Realtors, Americans for Quality Nursing Homes, and the American Medical Association were the only business groups that broadcast ads to help Democrats. Further, these three business groups targeted their efforts to help few beneficiaries: Democratic representatives Cal Dooley of California, James Maloney of Connecticut and challenger Scotty Baesler of Kentucky. Challenger Mark Dayton of Minnesota was the sole Democratic Senate candidate to receive business assistance in the upper chamber. Business interests aired roughly half of their spots in House races to help incumbents involved in the most competitive races and another 22 percent to help incumbents in moderately competitive races. Some of these ads were used to shore-up a policy ally who appeared at risk during some point in the election, call public attention to the incumbent's position on an issue, or enable a group to ingratiate itself with a powerful lawmaker. Business issue advocacy spending in Senate races was more defensive in posture, and perhaps more access-oriented, than in House contests. Eighty-six percent of all business-sponsored ads in Senate races were broadcast to help Republican incumbents. Most of these were aired in very competitive contests.

Labor unions, by contrast, aired all of their ads to help Democrats. The majority of these were broadcast in connection with very competitive challenger and open-seat campaigns. Labor aired few spots in connection with Senate races, but its ad placement in elections for both chambers reflects its commitment to helping the Democrats regain control of the Congress. Ideology clearly trumped access when labor devised its issue ad strategy in 2000.

Liberal groups were responsible for most of the ideological interest group television ads broadcast in connection with the 2000 congressional elections. The vast majority of their ads intended to influence House races

TABLE 3.5 THE DISTRIBUTION OF INTEREST GROUP TELEVISION ADVERTISEMENTS IN THE 2000 CONGRESSIONAL ELECTIONS

	HOUSE				SENATE			
	BUSINESS	LABOR UNION	IDEOLOGICAL	PARTY LEADERSHIP	BUSINESS	LABOR UNION	IDEOLOGICAL	PARTY LEADERSHIP
Democrats								
Incumbents								
Very competitive	2%	3%	—	—	—	—	31%	—
Moderately competitive	—	—	—	—	—	—	—	—
Uncompetitive	—	1%	—	—	—	—	—	—
Challengers								
Very competitive	—	52%	32%	—	—	100%	52%	—
Moderately competitive	—	33%	26%	—	2%	—	—	—
Uncompetitive	—	2%	1%	—	—	—	—	—
Open-Seat candidates								
Very competitive	—	9%	16%	—	—	—	10%	—
Moderately competitive	—	—	8%	—	—	—	—	—
Uncompetitive	—	—	2%	—	—	—	—	—
Republicans								
Incumbents								
Very competitive	49%	—	—	—	81%	—	2%	—
Moderately competitive	22%	—	—	—	—	—	—	—
Uncompetitive	6%	—	11%	—	5%	—	5%	—
Challengers								
Very competitive	7%	—	—	30%	4%	—	—	—
Moderately competitive	2%	—	—	—	—	—	—	—
Uncompetitive	1%	—	—	—	2%	—	—	—
Open-Seat candidates								
Very competitive	7%	—	5%	70%	7%	—	—	26%
Moderately competitive	3%	—	—	—	—	—	—	74%
Uncompetitive	1%	—	—	—	—	—	—	—
Total ads	21,226	12,425	5,655	417	6,777	540	4,542	1,073

Note: See the notes for Table 3.4.
Source: Compiled from data provided by the Wisconsin Advertising Project.

were broadcast in very or moderately competitive contests. Ideological groups were more active in the reelection efforts of Democratic senators than Democratic House members, but most of their ads for elections in both chambers focused on Democratic challengers and open-seat contestants. Only two ideological groups—ALT and the League of Conservation Voters—ran ads for candidates of both parties.

Organizations affiliated with House party leaders' aired all of their issue ads in competitive nonincumbent contests. Leadership PAC advertising in Senate campaigns deviated from this pattern, since GOP leaders aired a large number of ads in the open-seat race in New York between First Lady Hillary Rodham Clinton and Republican representative Rick Lazio.

The elections between Chapin and Keller and Robb and Allen featured substantial interest group activity. The Florida Women Voters, a pro-choice group, broadcast 249 spots on behalf of Chapin, and the AFL-CIO aired another 113 ads. Keller received support from the Republican Leadership Council, which sponsored 249 ads, and the Association of Builders and Contractors, which aired another 176. In the Virginia Senate contest, the League of Conservation Voters and Voters for Choice, aired 666 and 543 ads, respectively, for Robb. Allen, whose campaign was much better financed than Robb's, was supported by the Chamber of Commerce, which ran 255 ads, and National Pro-Life Alliance, which ran 15 ads. Interest groups, like party committees, made their influence felt in close elections via the television airwaves.

THE TIMING OF CAMPAIGN ADS

Few party organizations become involved in congressional primaries because they recognize that if the candidate they support is defeated they will have created ill will with their party's nominee and probably will have harmed his or her prospects in the general election. Party committees prefer to stockpile their resources for use against the opposing parties' candidates. Many interest groups limit their participation in contested primaries for similar reasons. As a result, party committees and interest groups do not swamp the airwaves with television spots until after the nomination is decided. Parties aired no candidate-focused issue advocacy ads for the purposes of influencing 2000 House or Senate primaries. Interest groups aired roughly 1 percent—a total of 444 ads—to influence nominations for the House.[29] Americans for Limited Terms broadcast most of these. It aired 159 ads in the Ohio Republican primary contest to replace former representative John Kasich, where it backed term limits supporter state senator Eugene Watts. The ads praised Watts's military service and teaching experience, and portrayed his primary opponent, state representative Pat Tiberi as a shill for lobbyists and special interests.[30] Despite ALT's efforts Tiberi won the primary and the general election. ALT had more success in the Republican

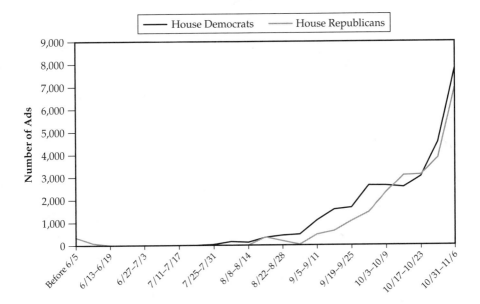

FIGURE 3.1   THE TIMING OF PARTY TELEVISION ADVERTISEMENTS IN THE 2000 HOUSE ELECTIONS

primary to replace Arizona representative Matt Salmon, who kept his promise to retire from Congress after serving three terms. The group aired 98 ads in support of Jeff Flake, the executive director of the Goldwater Institute, a conservative think tank, who won Salmon's endorsement as well as both the primary and the general election.[31]

Party committees held their fire in House campaigns until the general election season was well underway, indicating they invested few resources to set the national political agenda. This is typical for a presidential election year, where the presidential campaigns and national committees dominate the airwaves. Party ads in House races did not reach significant numbers until after the Labor Day weekend, the traditional start of the general election season (see Figure 3.1). The Democrats aired slightly more ads than the Republicans, but the timing of the parties' broadcasts shadowed one another.

Party advertising in Senate campaigns began to take off slightly earlier than it did in House contests (see Figure 3.2 on page 58). The Democrats began first, focusing most of their early spending on Mel Carnahan's campaign in Missouri and Hillary Clinton's race in New York. The GOP's advertising lagged somewhat behind the Democrats, both in quantity and in timing. However, both parties waited until September before airing large numbers of ads.

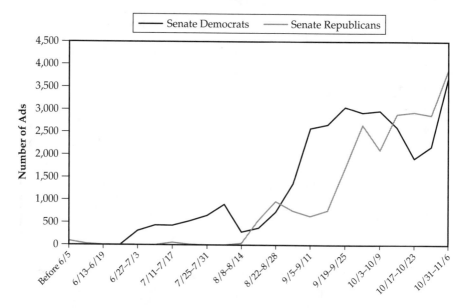

FIGURE 3.2   THE TIMING OF PARTY TELEVISION
ADVERTISEMENTS IN THE 2000 SENATE ELECTIONS

Business groups also waited until well into the general election season to air the lion's share of their issue ads, indicating that they made little effort to set the campaign agenda in most House races (see Figure 3.3). Ideological groups entered the fray somewhat earlier in order to become involved in a few primaries, but the timing of most of their ads suggests that they were mainly trying to influence the direction of later campaign dialogues that were already under way. Labor unions, on the other hand, set out early to influence the campaign agenda in several House races. They aired more than three-fourths of their ads prior to the traditional start of the election season, reserving few resources for the last month of the campaign. During this period, labor shifted tactics from the airwaves to the ground, using its paid organizers and volunteers to mobilize union members and their families.

Interest group activity in the 2000 Senate elections bears similarities and differences to that in the House races. Ideological groups were active early in the election season, including in some primaries, and later made their presence known on the airwaves in September (see Figure 3.4 on page 60). Business groups broadcast a substantial number of ads prior to the traditional Labor Day kickoff, but reserved most of their ads for the last three weeks of the election. Most of business's early advertising was intended to influence the Senate campaigns of Spencer Abraham in Michigan, who received strong

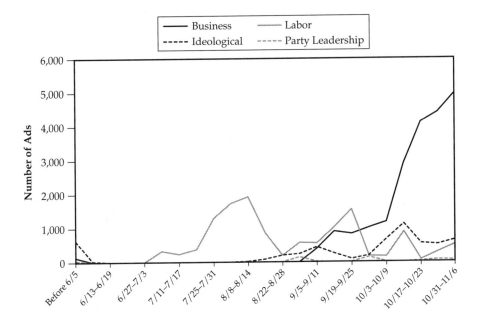

FIGURE 3.3   THE TIMING OF INTEREST GROUP TELEVISION
ADVERTISEMENTS IN THE 2000 HOUSE ELECTIONS

early support from the Business Roundtable and Americans for Job Security, and Rick Lazio in New York, who received solid early backing from the
Republican Leadership Council. In contrast to some campaigns for the lower
chamber, labor unions made no attempt to set the agenda in races for the Senate, waiting until the last three weeks of the election to take to the airwaves.
Party leadership PACs and other groups affiliated with party leaders were
relatively more active in elections for the Senate than the House. They spread
their efforts out across the campaign season.

THE FOCUS OF PARTY AND INTEREST GROUP ADS

The ads that candidates, parties, and interest groups televised for the purposes of influencing a congressional election covered a variety of issues.
Roughly one-quarter of all candidate and party ads broadcast in conjunction
with the 2000 congressional elections discussed the candidate's qualifications
and performance in office (see Table 3.6 on page 61 and Table 3.7 on page
62). The remainder focused on the economy and other policy issues. Most of
these issues, including social welfare, education, and the environment, traditionally have been favorably associated with the Democrats. Others, such
crime and drug prevention and government reform, have been positively associated with the GOP. The Republicans enjoyed an advantage on economic

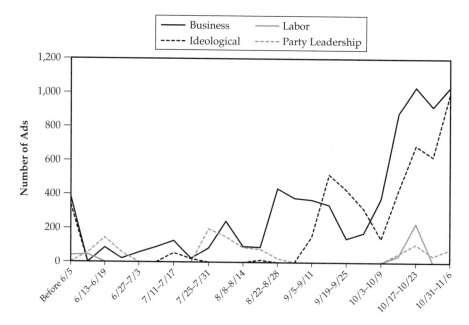

FIGURE 3.4   THE TIMING OF INTEREST GROUP TELEVISION
ADVERTISEMENTS IN THE 2000 SENATE ELECTIONS

issues during the Reagan era, but the economic progress made during the Clinton administration weakened the GOP's hold on that issue. Similarly, the forays of Republican governors, such as then-presidential candidate and governor of Texas George W. Bush and Wisconsin governor Tommy Thompson, into educational policy relaxed the Democrats' grip on education. Social issues, such as abortion rights, gun control, and tobacco have been and continue to be fair game for candidates of both parties. The overall aging of the New Deal party system weakened the holds of both parties on some of their traditional issues.[32]

The television ads broadcast during the 2000 congressional elections demonstrate that candidates and party committees ran ads on many of the same policy issues. Democratic candidates for the House and the Senate and Democratic party committees focused on social welfare concerns more than any other issue. The next most selected issue was education. Their Republican counterparts focused primarily on the economy and social welfare issues. Many interest groups did not air spots that focused on the same issues as did the parties and candidates. This is not surprising given that each interest group has its own issue agenda and, as noted earlier, groups use the electoral process to pursue a wider array of goals than do parties or candidates.

TABLE 3.6 ISSUES COVERED IN TELEVISION
ADVERTISEMENTS IN THE 2000 HOUSE ELECTIONS

	DEMOCRATS			REPUBLICANS		
	Candidate Ads	*Party Ads*	*Interest-Group Ads*	*Candidate Ads*	*Party Ads*	*Interest-Group Ads*
Candidate performance	22%	19%	9%	30%	28%	2%
Economic	8	5	1	20	27	2
Social welfare	35	42	61	19	12	79
Education	8	11	2	11	11	15
Social issue	6	6	7	3	2	1
Environment	3	2	2	2	1	—
Crime and drugs	2	1	—	1	4	—
Government reform	4	5	1	2	3	—
Foreign policy	1	—	—	1	2	—
Other	10	9	17	11	10	1
Total ads	74,022	28,930	18,102	69,769	23,917	22,348

Notes: "—" = less than 0.5%. Some columns may not add to 100 percent due to rounding. Includes only major-party candidates.

Source: Compiled from data provided by the Wisconsin Advertising Project.

Federal law prohibits parties and groups from directly coordinating televised issue advocacy efforts and independent expenditures with federal candidates. Nevertheless, informational exchanges of some sort undoubtedly took place, resulting in the parties and their candidates focusing on the same issues. It is not difficult for party committees or interest groups to learn the substance of a candidate's message. The Hill committees carefully track the progress made by their most competitive candidates and routinely provide them with strategic advice. They also take polls to learn about public reactions to candidates' campaigns. Some of these are shared with the candidate. Polls commissioned by news organizations serve a similar purpose. Moreover, the community of party officials, interest group leaders, professional consultants, and candidates involved in political campaigns is not very large, and it is only natural that some strategic information about specific campaigns flows among them, even if only indirectly.

THE TONE OF PARTY AND INTEREST GROUP ADS

Campaign ads are used for a variety of purposes. Positive ads promote a candidate by touting such things as the candidate's character, experience, job performance, or issue positions. Negative ads attack an opponent on some of

TABLE 3.7   ISSUES COVERED IN TELEVISION
ADVERTISEMENTS IN THE 2000 SENATE ELECTIONS

	DEMOCRATS			REPUBLICANS		
	CANDIDATE ADS	PARTY ADS	INTEREST GROUP ADS	CANDIDATE ADS	PARTY ADS	INTEREST GROUP ADS
Candidate performance	24%	24%	31%	33%	27%	12%
Economic	12	6	—	14	17	15
Social welfare	32	39	18	24	24	54
Education	11	10	24	10	8	3
Social issue	6	7	11	5	6	1
Environment	1	1	9	1	—	8
Crime and drugs	1	5	—	4	5	—
Government reform	4	5	4	2	6	—
Foreign policy	—	—	—	2	1	—
Other	8	4	3	4	6	7
Total ads	89,532	30,610	4,893	81,273	22,412	8,087

Notes: "—" = less than 0.5%. Some columns may not add to 100 percent due to rounding. Includes only major-party candidates. The figure for Senate Republicans includes 148 ads that New York's Conservative Party aired on behalf of Ric Lazio.

Source: Compiled from data provided by the Wisconsin Advertising Project.

TABLE 3.8   THE TONE OF TELEVISION
ADVERTISEMENTS IN THE 2000 CONGRESSIONAL ELECTIONS

	HOUSE			SENATE		
	CANDIDATE ADS	PARTY ADS	INTEREST GROUP ADS	CANDIDATE ADS	PARTY ADS	INTEREST GROUP ADS
Positive	56%	14%	32%	61%	11%	35%
Negative	17	68	64	14	53	56
Contrast	27	18	4	25	36	9
Total ads	143,791	52,847	40,450	170,805	53,022	12,980

Notes: Some columns may not add to 100 percent due to rounding. Includes only major-party candidates. The figure for Senate party ads includes 148 ads that New York's Conservative party aired on behalf of Rick Lazio.

Source: Compiled from data provided by the Wisconsin Advertising Project.

these same dimensions. Contrast ads make one candidate look good in comparison to an opponent.[33] Despite laws that prohibit the coordination of issue advocacy and independent expenditure ads, a de facto division of labor seems to have taken place in some 2000 congressional elections. Fifty-six percent of all House candidates' spots were positive, 17 percent were negative, and 27 percent contrasted both candidates (see Table 3.8 on page 62). The ads broadcast by parties and interest groups followed a very different pattern. All but 14 percent of the party ads were intended to show the opposing party's candidates in an unfavorable light, either by attacking the opponent or contrasting the opponent negatively with the party's own contestants. Interest group ads were somewhat less negative: Roughly one-third promoted an ally and two-thirds attacked an opponent. The patterns for Senate campaigns are similar except that the parties and groups aired more contrast than pure attack ads.

Democrat Elaine Bloom's bid for Florida's 22nd district seat is illustrative of an election where a division of responsibility appears to have taken place. Bloom, who had served eighteen years in the Florida legislature, was challenging nine-term Republican incumbent Clay Shaw (see box on page 64). Both candidates spent considerable funds in this hard-fought contest, with Shaw outspending Bloom $3.1 million to $2.4 million.[34] The Bloom campaign broadcast 1,751 individual spots. Roughly 80 percent of them were issue-oriented positive or contrast spots. Many focused on education and health care. The Democrats and the National Education Association (NEA) also focused on education. The Florida Democratic Party ran 940 spots, all of them negative, including some blasting Shaw's congressional voting record on education. Interest groups broadcast 1,251 spots: 90 percent of them were negative and 10 percent were contrast ads. They include 131 spots aired by the NEA contrasting the candidates on Head Start, teacher training, and other education issues.

There was less of a division of labor on the Republican side. Shaw broadcast 1,910 ads. Only 20 percent of these were positive or contrast spots. Most focused on senior citizens' issues. The remaining 80 percent were negative. The Florida Republican Party aired 498 spots, all of them negative. Most attacked Bloom for her role as director of a pharmaceutical company. Interest groups accounted for another 1,568 ads designed to help Shaw. Forty-one percent of them, including ads aired by the U.S. Chamber of Congress, were negative. The remaining interest group spots were positive ads broadcast by the American Medical Association.

Both parties and interest groups used issue advocacy advertising to make their presence felt in the Shaw-Bloom election. They accounted for 54 percent of the total number of spots broadcast in connection with the race. It is impossible to credit any one factor with determining the outcome of the elections, but the outside spending by these organizations undoubtedly had an impact on many voters' perceptions of the candidates, and may have influenced the outcome of the race. It probably contributed to Shaw's 596-vote victory margin.

Issue advocacy advertising in the Virginia Senate race also largely freed the candidates from having to broadcast negative ads (see box on page 65). Robb's ads focused on a variety of traditional Democratic issues, including

TELEVISION ADVERTISEMENTS IN FLORIDA'S TWENTY-SECOND DISTRICT

Positive Ad Sponsored by Elaine Bloom for Congress

Announcer: Over 100 laws. After 18 years as a state representative Elaine Bloom has written and passed over 100 laws helping South Florida. Raising teacher standards, more alternatives to nursing homes, healthcare for the uninsured, a concealed weapons ban, smaller class sizes, no smoking sections, increased exports, home healthcare. Imagine all she could do in Congress. Democrat Elaine Bloom, our priorities.

Attack Ad Sponsored by Florida Democratic Party

Announcer: Here's the deal. In 1995, Clay Shaw voted to make Newt Gingrich Speaker of the House. Then Shaw received a new chairmanship. Since then, Clay Shaw's voted nearly 90 percent of the time with Republican leaders, voting against hiring 100,000 new teachers, and against smaller class sizes. Voting to cut student loans by $10 billion, even voting to eliminate the Department of Education. Tell Clay Shaw his deal with Republican leaders is a raw deal for our kids.

Contrast Ad Sponsored by National Education Association

Announcer: As the teachers of NEA, we know what's at stake in our schools. And Elaine Bloom has fought for our children's education her whole career. In Congress, she'll stand for Head Start for every eligible child, for smaller class size, and for increased teacher training. In Congress, Clay Shaw voted no to Head Start, no to smaller class size, and no to teacher training. The difference is clear. Elaine Bloom for Congress.

Positive Ad Sponsored by the Committee to Re-Elect Shaw

Announcer: It wasn't fair. Washington was taking social security away from working seniors.
Shaw: Congress was penalizing those that had to continue to work. That was wrong.
Announcer: When Clay Shaw became Chairman of the Social Security Committee, he stopped Washington's unfair earnings penalties on seniors. Then Shaw passed legislation to keep social security funds safe, in a lockbox, away from big spending politicians. He's protecting social security. South Florida's senior Congressman. Clay Shaw.

Attack Ad Sponsored by Republican Party of Florida

Announcer: While she attacks Clay Shaw and prescription drugs, Elaine Bloom knows in her heart that she's the one cheating seniors. As a director of a company making a heart medication, Elaine Bloom's part of the team that acted to keep drug prices officially high. Elaine Bloom could have stood up for seniors and lowered drug prices but she didn't. Instead her company made millions. Call Elaine Bloom. Tell her it's not right for us, senior citizens, to choose between the medications we need and the food we eat.

Attack Ad Sponsored by the U.S. Chamber of Commerce

Man: I heard Elaine Bloom supports this White House prescription drug plan for seniors. What happens to the good prescription drug plan that I already have through my company retirement? They say I could lose it, and be left with this government plan that may cost more and have fewer benefits. And whose gonna run this big government plan? Will some bureaucrat be telling me what kind of medicine I can have?
Announcer: Tell Elaine Bloom to stop scaring seniors. Stop supporting the White House prescription drug plan.

Source: Wisconsin Advertising Project.

TELEVISION ADVERTISEMENTS IN VIRGINIA'S SENATE RACE

Positive Ad Sponsored by Robb for Senate

Announcer: He answered to his call. Volunteered for combat and lead a company of Marines in Vietnam. Back home in Virginia, he became the Education Governor. In the Senate, he has reached across party lines. Supporting President Bush on a majority of his initiatives. And joining bipartisan efforts to cut spending and balance the budget. Pro-choice. For the Death Penalty and for a strong national defense. Now he's fighting to modernize our schools, reduce class sizes, and for a prescription drug benefit for seniors. Senator Robb when duty calls.

Attack Ad Sponsored by the Democratic Party of Virginia

Johnson: I'm a former Virginia college president. I know George Allen's record on education and I want you to know the facts. As Congressman, he tried to cut the Department of Education. As Governor, he vetoed class size reduction and he proposed a budget to cut nearly $100 million from Virginia schools. $47 million from colleges and universities. Even Republican's said Allen's cuts in education went too far. To check the facts about George Allen's record for yourself, visit this Web site: <theallenrecord.com>.

Contrast Ad Sponsored by Voters for Choice

Couric: I'm Emily Couric. As a woman in public life, I've always supported a woman's right to make her own reproductive healthcare decisions. That is why I hope you pay special attention to the candidates for U.S. Senate. Chuck Robb has been a champion for a woman's right to choose but his opponent George Allen said he would roll back Roe versus Wade and restrict the right, even in the first months of pregnancy. Check the record. Chuck Robb will protect our rights. George Allen won't.

Positive Ad Sponsored by Friends of George Allen

Announcer: He's been called one of the most influential Governors in recent Virginia history. With a record that includes abolishing parole, taking people from welfare to work and investing in our schools. And he did it all while cutting taxes and creating over 300,000 new jobs. In the Senate, he'll keep working for excellence in education, lower taxes on working families and cracking down on pushers who sell drugs to our children. George Allen. Proven leadership and Virginia values in the Senate.

Attack Ad Sponsored by the U.S. Chamber of Commerce

Announcer: Senator Robb supports a big-government prescription drug plan that could be costly for seniors. This plan requires seniors to pay up to $600 a year plus 50/50 co-payment. In this big-government plan, seniors have a one time chance to sign up, otherwise they face penalties to join later. And who would decide which medicines are covered and which aren't? Tell Senator Robb to stop scaring seniors. Tell him to stop supporting a big-government prescription drug plan.

Contrast Ad Sponsored by Republican Party of Virginia

Announcer: The facts on gun violence: George Allen abolished parole for criminals who commit gun violence. Chuck Robb doubled parole for criminals, increasing violent crime. George Allen went to court to expel violent students who bring guns to school. Robb voted against expelling students with guns. George Allen pushed instant background checks for all guns. Police across Virginia stand with George Allen to keep gun violence out of our neighborhoods and schools. George Allen's record has made Virginia safer.

Source: Wisconsin Advertising Project.

education, prescription drug benefits, and abortion rights. Roughly 40 percent were purely positive spots; the remainder were contrast ads. More than two-thirds of the commercials broadcast by the Virginia Democratic Party attacked Allen, and the remainder made unfavorable contrasts between Robb and him on pro-Democratic issues. Interest group spots intended to help Robb were somewhat more evenly divided between negative and contrast ads, but none of them were positive. The Allen campaign was similar to the Robb campaign in that most of its spots were positive or contrast ads.[35] They focused on crime prevention, tax cuts, and a variety of other issues that are favorably associated with the GOP. Republican party committees ran contrast and negative ads to improve Allen's and detract from Robb's standing on these issues. The Chamber of Commerce and the National Pro-Life Alliance were the only pro-Allen groups to run ads in the contest. The former sought to undermine Robb's credibility on prescription drug benefits for senior citizens; the latter attacked him for his support of abortion rights. Party committees and interest groups accounted for 53 percent of the spots aired. They influenced the tenor of the election and may have helped to produce its outcome.

CONCLUSION

The advent of issue advocacy advertising has had a major impact on the roles of political parties and interest groups in congressional elections. In 2000 these organizations aired a substantial number of the television spots in many close House and Senate elections, occasionally broadcasting a greater number of campaign ads than the candidates themselves. The coincidence of the substantive content of some party, candidate, and interest group ads, and what appears to be a de facto division of responsibility regarding attacking an opponent, suggests that there is at least some informal exchange of strategic information among candidates and these other organizations. Party and interest group issue advocacy has changed the dynamics of some hotly contested congressional campaigns and probably altered the outcomes of some elections.

Party and interest group efforts in 2000 changed the dynamic of candidate-centered elections somewhat in the closest congressional elections. Candidates in these races did not dominate the television airwaves, radio frequencies, direct mail, or the other communications media in their districts, as did most other candidates in 2000 and did most candidates of an earlier era. The fact that most parties and groups tailored their ads to specific House and Senate contests, suggests that outside spending, like most other aspects of congressional elections, remain candidate-focused rather than party-oriented. The rise of issue advocacy advertising has a downside for voters and candidates. Campaigning by parties and interest groups can make it difficult for voters to hold candidates accountable for the substance of their campaigns or their performance in office. This is particularly true when parties and groups air attack or comparative spots that misrepresent a candidate's record. Such campaigning, when presented in the form of personal attacks on a candidate, also can discourage citizens' trust in government and demobilize voters. It does little to enhance representation in Congress or to increase the legitimacy of the political system. Television issue advocacy has increased the influence of parties and interest groups in elections, but it is questionable as to whether it has improved elections or the governmental process more generally.

APPENDIX

The coding of most but not all of the variables used to analyze the CMAG data is self-explanatory.

Interest groups were categorized as follows:

Business groups includes organizations sponsored by corporations, other businesses, and trade associations, such as the Business Round Table, U.S. Chamber of Commerce, Association of Builders and Contractors, American Medical Association, Citizens for Better Medicare, and Americans for Quality Nursing Home Care.

Ideological groups includes nonconnected committees, such as the League of Conservation Voters, U.S. Term Limits, EMILY's List, Voters for Choice, and Planned Parenthood.

Labor unions include labor organizations, such as the AFL-CIO and NEA.

Party leadership groups include organizations associated with party leaders, such as the Republican Leadership Council.

Issues were categorized as follows:

Candidate performance includes references to the candidate's attendance record, political record, personal values, or integrity.

Crime and drugs includes references to crime, illegal drugs, death penalty, other reference to law and order.

Economics includes references to taxes, the deficit, budget, government debt, government spending, trade, specific economic sectors (e.g., farming), and other economic issues.

Education includes all references to education.

Environment includes all references to the environment.

Foreign policy includes references to defense, antiballistic missiles/ Star Wars, veterans, foreign policy, other defense and foreign policy issues.

Government reform includes references to campaign finance reform, government ethics, and special interests.

Social issues includes references to abortion, homosexuality, moral values, tobacco, affirmative action, gambling, assisted suicide, gun control, civil rights, race relations, and other social issues.

Social welfare includes references to the minimum wage, employment/ jobs, poverty, health care, Social Security, Medicare, welfare, childcare, and other child-related issues.

Other includes a small group of miscellaneous issues.

NOTES

1. A small portion of this spending was on televised independent expenditure ads. This figure underestimates the parties' and groups' actual expenditures because it only includes media buys (not production costs), only includes spending in the nation's 75 largest media markets (excluding 135 smaller markets), and is based on television stations' published rates rather than the actual charges levied by the stations, which were inflated as the election date approached. The figure is calculated from CMAG data.

2. Paul S. Herrnson, *Party Campaigning in the 1980s*, 18–29; *Congressional Elections*, 84–85.

3. Paul S. Herrnson, *Party Campaigning in the 1980s*, 47–111; *Congressional Elections*, 100–111, 129–140.

4. A small portion of this spending was on televised independent expenditure ads. This figure underestimates the parties' and groups' actual expenditures because it only includes media buys (not production costs), only includes spending in the nation's 75 largest media markets (excluding 135 smaller markets), and is based on television stations' published rates rather than the actual charges levied by the stations, which were inflated as the election date approached. The figure is calculated from CMAG data.

5. Paul S. Herrnson, *Party Campaigning in the 1980s* (Cambridge: Harvard University Press), 31–111.

6. Paul S. Herrnson, *Congressional Elections: Campaigning at Home and in Washington* (Washington, D.C.: CQ Press, 2000), 92.

7. Sen. Mitch McConnell, R-KY., quoted on *Face the Nation*, November 1, 1998.

8. Gary C. Jacobson and Samuel Kernell, *Strategy and Choice in Congressional Elections* (New Haven, CT: Yale University Press, 1983), 39–43, 76–84.

9. During the final weeks of the 2000 election most pundits believed that about forty House races would be competitive, far fewer than in previous years. On 2000, see Paul S. Herrnson "The Congressional Elections," in *The Election of 2000*, ed. Gerald M. Pomper. (Chatham, NJ: Chatham House, 2001), 162. On previous years see Herrnson, *Congressional Elections*, 91.

10. See, for example, Gregory M. Saltzman, "Congressional Voting on Labor Issues: The Role of PACs," *Industrial and Labor Relations Review* 40 (1987): 263–279.

11. See J. David Gopoian, "What Makes PACs Tick? An Analysis of the Allocation Patterns of Economic Interest Groups," *American Journal of Political Science* 28 (May 1984): 259–281; Craig Humphries, "Corporations, PACs, and the Strategic Link between Contributions and Lobbying Activities," *Western Political Quarterly* 44 (1991): 353–372; Frank J. Sorauf, *Inside Campaign Finance* (New Haven, CT: Yale University Press, 1992), 64–65, 74–75; and the case

studies in *After the Revolution: PACs, Lobbies, and the Republican Congress*, ed. Robert Biersack, Paul S. Herrnson, and Clyde Wilcox (Boston: Allyn and Bacon, 1999).

12. Some party assistance is provided to candidates in the form of coordinated expenditures that are made on behalf of candidates. Parties and interest groups also provide candidates with "in kind" contributions of campaign services.

13. See, for example, Anthony Corrado, Thomas E. Mann, Daniel R. Ortiz, Trevor Potter, and Frank J. Sorauf, eds., *Campaign Finance: A Sourcebook* (Washington, D.C.: Brookings Institution, 1997).

14. On the concept of party issue ownership, see John R. Petrocik, "Issue Ownership in Presidential Elections, with a 1980 Case Study," *American Journal of Political Science* 40(1996): 825–850.

15. Paul S. Herrnson and Diana Dwyre, "Party Issue Advocacy in Congressional Elections," in *The State of the Parties*, 3rd ed., ed. John C. Green and Daniel M. Shea (Lanham, MD: University Press of America, 1999), 86–104. See the case studies in *Outside Money: Soft Money and Issue Advocacy in the 1998 Congressional Elections*, ed. David B. Magleby (Lanham, MD: Rowman and Littlefield, 2000).

16. Ibid.

17. The remainder of the elections took place in the 145 smaller media markets for which CMAG did not collect data. The CMAG data are discussed in greater detail in the introduction to this volume.

18. As discussed in Note 1, CMAG estimates for the costs of television ads are based on stations' published rates rather than the actual charges levied by the stations, which were inflated as the election date approached. The Pearson correlation between the frequency of party and interest group ads designed to help a House campaign and the amounts these organizations spent on those ads is .77. The correlation for Senate campaigns is .94.

19. The budgetary figures are based on all major-party general election candidates, including those who did not broadcast television commercials. See Herrnson, *Congressional Elections*, 81–82, 205.

20. Herrnson, *Party Campaigning in the 1980s*, 60.

21. Mark J. Rozell and Clyde Wilcox, *Interest Groups in American Campaigns* (Washington, D.C.: CQ Press, 2000), 157.

22. See "Party Soft Money," Anthony Corrado, in Corrado, et al., *Campaign Finance*, 167–177, and Trevor Potter, "Issue Advocacy and Express Advocacy," in Corrado, et al., *Campaign Finance*, 227–239, and Herrnson, *Congressional Elections*, 15–19.

23. Herrnson, *Congressional Elections*, 232–237; also see the case studies in Magleby, *Outside Money*.

24. Herrnson, *Congressional Elections*, 114–115.

25. Herrnson, *Congressional Elections*, 95–97, 113–115.

26. Center for Responsive Politics, Web site <http://www.opensecrets.org/2000elect/dist_total/FL08.htm>.

27. Center for Responsive Politics, Web site <http://www.opensecrets.org/2000elect/dist_total/VAS1.htm>.

28. Herrnson, *Congressional Elections*, 133–137, 142–143.

29. Herrnson, *Congressional Elections*, 134.

30. Figures compiled from CMAG data. Interest groups did not broadcast any ads in connection with the primaries of Senate elections included in the top seventy-five media markets.

31. Eddie Taylor, "The Fight over Kasich's Seat," unpublished paper, December 2000.

32. Emily Pierce, "Open Seat Profile: Arizona 1st District," *Congressional Quarterly*, November 10, 1999, Web site <http://www.washingtonpost.com/wp-dyn/politics/elections/2000/states/az/house/az01/A5002-1999Nov15.html>.

33. See for example, Martin P. Wattenberg, "The Hollow Realignment: Partisan Change in a Candidate Centered Era," *Public Opinion Quarterly* 51 (1987): 58–74; George Rabinowitz, Paul-Henri Gurian, and Stuart Elaine MacDonald, "The Structure of Presidential Elections and the Process of Realignment, 1944 to 1980," *American Journal of Political Science*, 28(1984): 611–635; and John R. Petrocik, "Realignment: New Party Coalitions and the Nationalization of the South," *Journal of Politics* 49(1987): 347–375.

34. On attack and contrast ads see, for example, Stephen Ansolabehere, Shanto Iyengar, Adam Simon, and Nicholas Valentino, "Does Attack Advertising Demobilize the Electorate?"

American Political Science Review 88(1994): 892–938; Richard R. Lau, Lee Sigelman, Caroline Heldman, and Paul R. Rabbit, "The Effects of Negative Political Advertisements: A Meta-Analytic Assessment," *American Political Science Review* 93(1999): 851–876; and Kathleen Hall Jamieson, Paul Waldman, and Susan Sherr, "Eliminate the Negative? Categories for Analysis of Political Advertisements," in *Crowded Airwaves: Campaign Advertising in Elections*, ed. James Thurber, Candice J. Nelson, and David A. Dulio (Washington, D.C.: Brookings Institution Press, 2000), 44–64.

35. Center for Responsive Politics, Web site <http://www.opensecrets.org/2000elect/dist_total/FL22.htm>.

THE ELECTORAL IMPACT OF "ISSUE ADVOCACY" IN 1998 AND 2000 HOUSE RACES

JONATHAN S. KRASNO[1]

B ehind the polite fiction that issue advocacy promotes issues is the universally understood, if not always acknowledged, fact that most of these ads are intended exclusively to aid particular candidates. Do they succeed?

On one hand, that might seem like a silly question given the hundreds of millions of dollars spent on issue advocacy in the last two election cycles. It is hard to imagine this money wasted, especially since most of it was spent by political parties, organizations with apparent expertise in electioneering. Even interest groups with less experience in campaigning use paid political consultants to design and place their advertisements, often the same consultants employed by the candidates.

On the other hand, there are at least several reasons to suspect the effectiveness of issue ads. To begin with, they are, at least by comparison to ads sponsored by candidates, somewhat restricted in the language they may use. And, since they emanate from a variety of party organizations and groups, it is easy to imagine that their messages might not fit perfectly with the campaigns waged by their favored candidates, thereby reducing their impact on voters.[2]

Neither of these factors turns out to be of much concern. While it is true that issue ads may not directly exhort viewers to "vote for" or "defeat" a particular candidate, even ads aired by candidates, free to use whatever language they like, rarely employ the so-called "magic words" of express advocacy (Krasno and Goldstein 2002).[3] Instead, candidates are content to trumpet their own virtues (like commercial advertisers) or disparage their opponents (less like commercial advertisers), leaving it to viewers to draw their own conclusions about what actions to take. Similarly, there is little sign of thematic disparity between issue ads, particularly those run in the final weeks of the campaign, and traditional electioneering (Krasno and Seltz 2000).

In theory then, issue advertising should be every bit as effective as money spent by the candidates' themselves and the millions of dollars spent on televised issue ads in 1998 and 2000 should have had a substantial influence on election outcomes (e.g., Goldstein and Freedman 2000). Thanks to the quality of the CMAG data, this theory is now testable. In this chapter, I examine the marginal impact—the return from each increment of spending—of expenditures on issue advocacy on the vote in incumbent-contested House elections, using a simple statistical model that controls for spending by the candidates and the underlying partisanship of the district.

The results suggest that issue advertising did not work as well as spending by incumbents and challengers in the last two House elections. It is unclear, however, whether this difference reflects some inherent inefficiency in issue advocacy or whether it results from the particular strategy adopted by issue advertisers to concentrate their spending almost exclusively in the most hotly contested races in the country. The decision by issue advertisers to focus on this handful of elections directly leads to an even more surprising result that the net impact of issue advocacy in 1998 and 2000 was minimal. This finding holds up even when issue advocacy is assumed to be every bit as effective as campaign spending by candidates. The bottom line is that there is little evidence that issue advocacy played a pivotal role in more than a couple of the races studied here, a conclusion that calls into question the millions of dollars devoted to these advertisements.

ISSUE ADVOCACY IN 1998 AND 2000

The CMAG system tracks political commercials broadcast in the nation's top seventy-five media markets, seen by nearly 80 percent of U.S. households. CMAG's technology creates a "storyboard," the full text and a frame of video every five seconds, of each ad broadcast, along with the date, time, and station on which it aired. It also provides estimates of the cost of the airtime, based on the average prices paid during the time slot in which it appeared. Campaign advertisers, unlike most commercial advertisers, are virtual captives of the calendar and are willing in some cases to pay premium prices to insure their spots air precisely when they should (Magleby 2000). As a result, the CMAG cost estimates are almost certainly low, although they do provide an accurate gauge of the scope of issue advertising in different House districts.

In 1998, candidates, parties, and interest groups purchased airtime for more 277,000 spots to promote House or Senate candidates at an estimated cost approaching $163 million. In 2000, the massive amount of advertising in the presidential election helped fuel a virtual explosion in advertising that pushed the number of commercials aired for federal candidates in the top seventy-five markets to 770,000 and estimated spending above $563 million.[4] Most of these ads came from candidates (82 percent in 1998 and 55 percent in 2000), leaving spending by parties and groups at $28 million in 1998 and $242 million in 2000.[5] Virtually all of the parties' and groups' commercials were issue ads in both years. Figure 4.1 breaks down the spending on airtime in both years by advertiser and by type of race. Senate races were the most popular subject of political ads in both years and congressional contests the least—a pattern that reflects the inefficiency of the largest media markets for House candidates (e.g., Krasno and Seltz 2000, 114).

Looking only at commercials for House candidates still leaves a substantial number of spots. About two-thirds of the 360,000 ads and estimated $221 million spent on airtime in 1998 and 2000 came from the candidates themselves. Naturally, incumbents were the most profligate of candidates ($61 million), though challengers were not as far behind ($38 million) as the even more wildly lopsided Federal Election Commission (FEC) figures would suggest. The reason is probably that television advertising is not a ubiquitous feature in all House races, just in the most expensive ones where both sides are likely to have serious resources. Parties and groups invested nearly equal amounts in supporting challengers and incumbents across the districts monitored by CMAG, though obviously some candidates fared better than others. The vast majority of commercials sponsored by parties and groups in both years were issue ads, though there was a smattering of spots

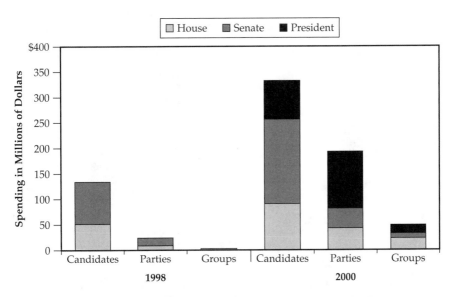

FIGURE 4.1   TV SPENDING BY ADVERTISER, 1998 AND 2000

that fell into two other campaign finance categories, coordinated expenditures and independent expenditures.[6] Figure 4.2 shows the distribution of spending by candidates, parties, and interest groups for incumbents, challengers, and candidates for open seats.

The media markets monitored by CMAG reach at least half of the households in more than 335 House districts, but advertisements for congressional candidates appeared in far fewer districts during either year (156 in 1998, 179 in 2000).[7] Foregoing television in many campaigns makes sense since only a fraction of House races are competitive. Candidates were by far the most active advertisers, sponsoring commercials in 144 districts in 1998 and 169 districts in 2000. Parties and interest groups were much pickier, running ads in about a third as many districts as candidates (64 in 1998, 62 in 2000). Obviously, there was tremendous overlap among the different advertisers. Neither parties nor groups ran ads in many districts ignored by candidates. What really stands out about issue advertising in both years, however, was its tight concentration in a handful of districts. In both years, at least half of all issue ads appeared in just twelve congressional districts.[8] These districts featured some of the highest-spending candidates in the country, although in some cases the candidates purchased fewer television spots than their allies did.

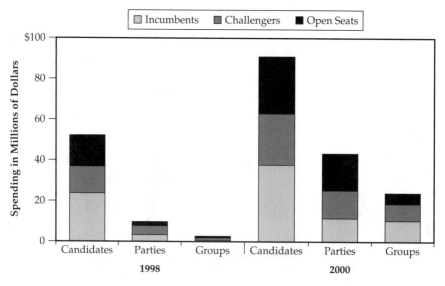

FIGURE 4.2   TV SPENDING IN HOUSE RACES BY ADVERTISER, 1998 AND 2000

THE IMPACT OF ISSUE ADS

Congressional elections are complex events. Dozens of different factors, some observable and some not, may contribute to the outcome in each district. Campaign spending, assumed to be so important by journalists, activists, and politicians, surely influences the vote. Measuring its impact accurately, however, requires taking the circumstances of each election into account.

To do so, I begin with a simple model of the House vote first developed by Professor Gary Jacobson in which the challenger's share of the two-party vote is a function of four factors: the challenger's vote share in the previous election, the challenger's party, the challenger's campaign spending, and the incumbent's campaign spending (Jacobson 1978).[9]

Previous vote share controls for the long-term partisan balance in the district, tempered by the popularity of the incumbent. Challenger's party is a dummy variable (measured 0 for Republicans and 1 for Democrats) that captures short-term tides that favor one party or another, such as the effect of Watergate in 1974 or the pro-Republican surge in 1994. Candidate spending figures come from the Federal Election Commission. In theory, controlling for all these variables will result in unbiased estimates of the marginal impact of each campaign dollar spent—at least before 1996 when issue advocacy began to play a large role in some House elections.

In practice, however, there are at least two additional matters to attend to. First is diminishing marginal returns, or the drop-off in the effectiveness of campaign spending at high levels. This is partly the result of saturation since the twentieth time that one hears the stirring story of a how a particular candidate is loved by their spouse, fought against taxes, or has worked hard for seniors is likely to be less powerful than the first. It is also due to the shrinking audience that campaigns encounter. Each candidate begins with a base of actual or potential supporters along with voters who are more difficult to win over. Candidates' initial spending, whether by design or not, often serves to activate their base, informing partisans about who the standard-bearer is and why they deserve support. These natural supporters are the first to come aboard and the easiest to convince, leaving a campaign to reach out to a less sympathetic and a less attentive portion of the electorate. The consequence is that marginal impact of campaign spending tails off after the early, dramatic gains. To account for this decline, I use the natural logarithm to transform candidate spending, a standard technique in this sort of analysis (Green and Krasno 1988, 1990; Jacobson 1978).

The greater difficulty is with the impact of incumbent spending. Incumbents, as successful political figures and almost certain winners, have extraordinary ability to raise funds. Most rarely have reason to use their ability fully; their opponents offer little challenge, little incentive for incumbents to strain themselves searching for every dollar they can find.[10] But they do utilize their financial capability when the circumstances demand it: when the electoral threat is greatest. The result is a paradox. The more incumbents spend, the worse they do. Correcting for this bias would be simple if we knew everything that incumbents know when they make their decisions.[11] Unfortunately, some of these considerations are unobservable. Political scientists have attempted to address this in a number of ways. My solution is to use incumbent spending from the previous election to purge current spending of bias (Green and Krasno 1988, 1990; Bartels 1991).

Since the model requires data from both the current and previous election, one regrettable side effect is that it limits usable cases to seats where the incumbent faced a major-party challenger in successive elections. Nevertheless, I am left with 465 total seats from 1998 and 2000, including 390 where at least 35 percent of residents lived within a media market monitored by CMAG. Parties and interest groups spent a substantial amount on airtime in these districts, $29 million (in 2000 dollars) for 37 incumbents and 43 challengers.[12]

This model produces estimates of the impact of candidate spending that are relatively stable, sizable, and properly signed for each election from 1978 to the present, as Figure 4.3 shows. So an incumbent who spent $500,000 (in 2000 dollars) received just under 4 percentage points of the two-party vote for her spending, compared to an extra 9 points for a challenger with the same spending.[13] Most incumbents were able to make up for this difference in productivity by outspending their opponents by substantial amounts. Incumbent

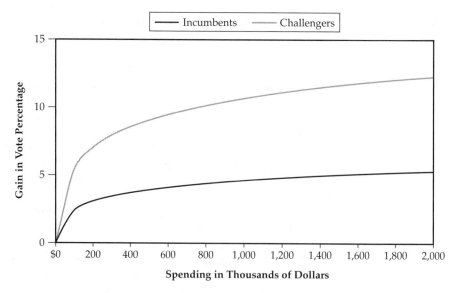

FIGURE 4.3   THE RETURN FROM CAMPAIGN SPENDING

expenditures were at least $250,000 higher than their challengers' in more than 80 percent of the races analyzed here; just 4 percent of these challengers managed to raise and spend more than their opponents. Figure 4.3 makes clear, however, that the effect of any disparity in spending depends on the level of expenditures in the contest. Because of diminishing marginal returns, the differential impact between spending $100,000 and $200,000 for both candidates is about equivalent to the gap between $1,000,000 and $2,000,000.

To estimate the effect of issue ads, I applied the same logarithmic transformation to CMAG data for the cost of airtime for these commercials and added these measures to the same model. Controlling for issue ads had little influence on the estimated effect of candidate spending. Figure 4.4 does reveal the more unexpected news that issue advocacy spending was notably less effective than candidate expenditures. For example, $500,000 in expenditures yielded an extra nine percentage points of the vote for challengers and about four points for incumbents, but the same amount of spending on issue ads added slightly over two points to challengers' vote and a half point to incumbents' share. This is especially noteworthy because the estimates of spending on issue advocacy are almost certainly low, since they do not reflect likely inflation in the cost of airtime near Election Day or the administrative and production costs incurred by the advertisers.[14] As a result, the spending curves in Figure 4.4 actually overestimate the true marginal impact of issue advocacy in this model.

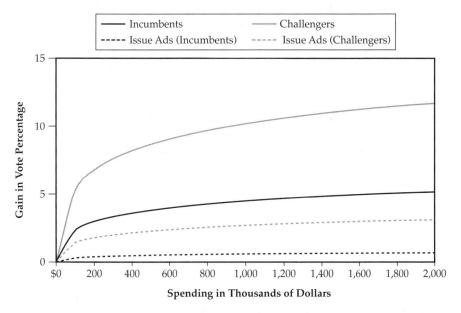

FIGURE 4.4   THE MARGINAL IMPACT OF ISSUE ADS

Is it possible that spending on issue advocacy by parties and interest groups is just a fraction as effective as campaign spending by candidates? As I mentioned earlier, there is little apparent difference in the content of television ads sponsored by candidates and issue advertisers. Surveys show that viewers do not recognize any distinction between campaign and issue ads (Magleby 2001). One possible explanation simply may be that television is an ineffective way of campaigning. If that is true, then the impact of candidate spending in this analysis is higher because it includes all expenditures—even costs like fundraising with zero electoral payoff—not just television. This hypothesis, so contrary to the conventional wisdom, could be tested using CMAG data but is beyond the scope of this chapter.

There are also several methodological explanations for this finding. One is that issue advocacy, like incumbent spending, is related to unobserved factors correlated with the vote. For example, parties and interest groups use polling to help them fine-tune their decisions where to invest their resources. If those polls pick up information not reflected in other variables in the model, I could be underestimating the impact of issue ads. This problem is likely alleviated by controlling for spending by the candidates and other issue advocates, factors frequently cited as influencing decisions of parties and interest groups to intervene in elections (Magleby 2000).[15] It is not clear how to correct further for this bias, if it indeed exists. But an even more straightforward explanation involves the distribution of issue advocacy dollars. Candidates spend funds in every district in the nation, from the most to the least competitive. Issue advocates, on the other hand, mainly restrict their involvement to just a handful of the tightest races. The result is issue advocacy spending provides relatively little traction for explaining variations in the House vote.[16] That is especially true because issue ads are most likely to appear in districts that are already heavily saturated with campaign propaganda from the candidates and where returns from spending are vastly diminished. In short, the effect of issue ads may be somewhat obscured by the narrow strategies adopted by their sponsors. In that case, survey data may offer a more accurate gauge than election returns.

Issue advertisers, however, care less about the marginal impact of each dollar they spend than about the bottom line of whether their money helped their favored candidates win. Getting a candidate from 49.9 percent of the vote to just over 50 is the key, whether or not much money seems to be wasted. The first way to address this question is by comparing predicted challenger vote from the model with and without issue ads (e.g., Figure 4.4 versus Figure 4.3). The predicted vote in just 4 percent of cases moved more than one percentage point, though in two races this was sufficient to nudge the challenger's share of the vote just over 50 percent. No incumbents seemed to benefit enough from issue advocacy to turn a predicted loss into a victory, but few incumbents were in any danger of losing.[17]

Of course, this calculation depends on the assumption that, dollar for dollar, issue advocacy is worth just a fraction of campaign spending by the candidates. What if we were to ignore the results in Figure 4.4 and assume that money spent on issue ads were the equivalent of candidate expenditures? I tested this hypothesis by adding spending on issue ads to the expenditures of the candidate favored, then reestimating the same model. The resulting coefficients for candidate spending are extremely close to those shown in Figures 4.3 and 4.4 (pages 76–77). More to the point, however, the predicted vote with this version of the model again shows little net effect for issue ads: The result in just 3 percent of cases changed by more than one point and the same two incumbents were shown losing their winning margins. Even adding $29,000,000 spent on airtime for issue ads to candidates' totals had little influence on results. Again the obvious explanation is diminishing marginal returns. Average spending by twenty-seven challengers who benefited from at least $100,000 in issue ads was $1.2 million; average spending by the twenty-four incumbents backed by at least $100,000 worth of commercials by their allies was just under $2 million. Simply put, these candidates already had plenty of money before their allies piled on.

CONCLUSION

The results of this analysis show that, after taking the context of the race into account, the effect of 1998 and 2000's issue advocacy campaigns on incumbent-contested House races was minimal. This conclusion emerges both from an examination of the marginal impact of spending on issue advocacy as well as a calculation of its net effect under different assumptions. Both of these findings are vulnerable to methodological critiques, the former for its failure to correct for potential bias in estimating the influence of issue ads and the latter for its approach to diminishing marginal returns. Neither criticism can be rejected outright, but it is clear that the decision of 1998 and 2000's issue advocates to concentrate their spending in the most hotly contested House races severely limited the impact of their expenditures. By focusing so narrowly on the closest and costliest elections in the country, these advertisers plainly hoped to provide the decisive shove necessary to tip races already teetering on the edge in their direction. Under the circumstances, it is no surprise to find that their spending affected a small number of voters since those efforts were designed for situations in which a small number of undecided voters might win or lose an election.

What if issue advocates had cast a wider net in 1998 and 2000, trying to make more second-tier contests more competitive? It is possible that we would see healthier effects than those in Figures 4.3 and 4.4. Given issue advocates' unwillingness so far to adapt this broader strategy, individual-level data may be the appropriate setting in which to measure the marginal productivity of their ads versus candidates. Nevertheless, any new findings must take into account the political context of the election while calculating the net effect of issue advocacy. As we have seen, even if issue ads were every bit as effective as other campaign propaganda, their electoral impact depends on the settings in which they appear. The choice to participate mainly in the tightest races inevitably limits the impact of issue advocacy, making it contingent on candidates' ability to make their races close and issue advertisers' acumen in picking the closest elections for their spots.

Several other topics for future research also flow from this analysis. Using WiscAds data, there is opportunity to segregate candidates' spending on television from their other expenditures in order to gauge its effect. This would allow a more direct comparison to the marginal productivity of parties and groups' investment in airtime. In addition, the precise rate at which returns from campaign spending diminish warrants additional investigation. No one doubts that they do diminish, but today, when $1 million campaigns are commonplace, it necessary to give extra attention to spending in the upper reaches of today's budgets.

While the findings here are, as always, subject to some debate and refinement among experts, their policy consequences are fairly clear. First of all, contrary to some claims, there can be no doubt that issue ads do little to make House elections more competitive. They may succeed in educating voters about issues as their supporters contend, though it is implausible to imagine that they impart much more than the candidate ads they resemble. But given the heavy investment in just a handful of districts and the already high level of competition in those districts, there is no evidence supporting the argument that issue ads help make elections closer or that without them there would be fewer contested races. By various measures—incumbent reelection rate, margin of victory, the number of competitive races, and so on—House elections have grown less competitive, not more, as expenditures on issue advocacy have risen over the past few election cycles. In retrospect, it is apparent that issue advocacy may have perversely helped limit the number of close races by allowing parties and groups to lavish attention and resources on a relatively small number of contests.

This account also speaks to the broader argument over deregulating the system of financing campaigns, a favorite of some political scientists (Mann 2002) and many Republicans who have advanced it in Congress and through a series of lawsuits. Critics of FECA maintain that the law has made it difficult for everyone involved to raise and spend money for campaigns, strangling politics and politicians (Smith 2001). The result is the familiar litany of complaints against congressional elections: high incumbent reelection rates, lack of competition, low turnout, and so forth. Yet, thanks to issue advocacy and soft money, the last two election cycles have served as a limited test of deregulation. The results of this experiment are not too encouraging. Proponents will certainly argue that the de facto deregulation of parties and interest groups was not sufficient, that candidates also need to be unleashed from the fundraising strictures of FECA. But, as shown here, the failure of parties and interest groups to invest more widely and more wisely surely raises disquieting questions about deregulation. Parties' strategic decisions in House races should be of particular wonderment to political scientists and others (e.g., Jackson 1988) who have long viewed these organizations as the potential salvation for congressional elections. Whether the parties' actions over the last election cycles reflect surprising incompetence (Kolodny 2001) or capture by candidates (Krasno and Sorauf 1998) is unclear. What is clear is that, left to their own devices, parties and groups have done more to escalate the cost of campaigns than to increase the competitiveness of elections.

REFERENCES

Bartels, Larry M. "Instrumental and Quasi-Instrumental Variables." *American Journal of Political Science* 35 (1991): 777–800.

Buckley v. Valeo, 424 U.S. 1 (1976).

Green, Donald P., and Jonathan S. Krasno. "Salvation for the Spendthrift Incumbent: Reestimating the Effects of Campaign Spending in House Elections." *American Journal of Political Science* 32 (1988): 884–907.

Green, Donald P., and Jonathan S. Krasno. "Rebuttal to Jacobson's 'New Evidence for Old Arguments.'" *American Journal of Political Science* 34 (1990): 363–372.

Goldstein, Ken and Paul Freedman. "New Evidence for New Arguments: Money and Advertising in the 1996 Senate Elections." *Journal of Politics* 62: 1087–1118.

Jackson, Brooks. *Honest Graft: Big Money and the American Political Process.* New York: Knopf, 1988.

Jacobson, Gary C. The Effects of Campaign Spending in Congressional Elections. *American Political Science Review* 72 (1978): 469–491.

Jacobson, Gary C. *The Politics of Congressional Elections* 5th ed. New York: Longman, 2000.

Kolodny, Robin. CFI Cyber-Forum: "Parties under McCain-Feingold." <http://www.cfinst.org/parties/mf_responses.html>.

Krasno, Jonathan S., and Ken Goldstein. "The Facts about Television Advertising and the McCain-Feingold Bill." *PS* (forthcoming).

Krasno, Jonathan S., and Daniel Seltz. *Buying Time: Television Advertising in the 1998 Congressional Elections.* New York: Brennan Center for Justice, 2000.

Krasno, Jonathan S., and Frank Sorauf. "The Joys of Regulation: Making the 'New' American Parties Responsible." Available from authors.

La Raja, Ray, and Elizabeth Jarvis-Shean. "Assessing the Impact of a Ban on Soft Money: Party Soft Money Spending in the 2000 Elections." Berkeley, CA: Institute of Governmental Studies, 2001. <http://www.cfinst.org/parties/papers/laraja_softmoney.pdf>.

Magleby, David B, ed. *Outside Money: Soft Money and Issue Advocacy in the 1998 Congressional Elections.* New York: Rowman and Littlefield, 2000.

Magleby, David B. "Dictum Without Data: The Myth of Issue Advocacy and Party Building." Brigham Young University, 2001. <http://www.byu.edu/outsidemoney/dictum/index.html>.

Mann, Thomas E. "Political Science and Campaign Finance Reform: Knowledge, Politics, and Policy." Prepared for delivery at the 2002 Annual Meeting of the American Political Science Association, August 29–September 1, 2002.

Moramarco, Glenn. "Regulating Electioneering: Distinguishing between 'Express Advocacy' and 'Issue Advocacy.'" 2000. <http://www.brennancenter.org/resources/downloads/cfr5.pdf>.

Schram, Martin. *Speaking Freely: Former Members of Congress Talk About Money in Politics.* Washington: Center for Responsive Politics, 1995.

Smith, Bradley A. *Unfree Speech: The Folly of Campaign Finance Reform.* Princeton, NJ: Princeton University Press, 2001.

NOTES

1. I thank the Pew Charitable Trusts for funding this research and the Open Society Institute for their support of an earlier project on independent expenditures that informed this study. Data for this project come from the Wisconsin Advertising Project (WiscAd) and the Campaign Media Analysis Group.
2. The Supreme Court made this same point about independent expenditures in *Buckley* (p. 233): "Unlike contributions, such independent expenditures may well provide little assistance to the candidate's campaign and may indeed prove counterproductive. The absence of pre-arrangement and coordination of an expenditure with the candidate or his agent not only undermines the value of the contribution to the candidate, but also alleviates the danger that expenditures will be given as a quid pro quo for improper commitments from a candidate." In the case of issue ads, a greater degree of coordination is possible but not always achieved. For information about various groups sponsoring issue ads see the Annenberg Institute's Web site at <http://www.appcpenn.org/issueads/gindex.htm>.
3. In its attempt to limit the reach of the Federal Election Campaign Act to electioneering, the Supreme Court noted in a footnote that the "application of 608 [is restricted] to communications containing express words of advocacy of the election or defeat, such as 'vote for,' elect,' 'support,' 'cast your ballot for,' 'Smith for Congress,' 'vote against,' 'defeat,' 'reject.'" Subsequently, this sentence has come to be interpreted narrowly and literally by lower courts, creating the so-called "magic words" test—and the issue advocacy loophole (Moramarco 2000).
4. These are ads rated by coders as primarily intended to "generate support or opposition to a particular candidate." About 60 percent of issue ads sponsored by groups and nearly all sponsored by parties fell into this category in both 1998 and 2000.
5. Figure 4.1 confirms that a main reason for the surge in the percentage of ads run by parties and interest groups was the presidential campaign. Because candidate campaign committees must abide by spending limits (to collect the public subsidy), many expensive tasks are handled by the candidates' allies.
6. Coordinated and independent expenditures can be determined in most cases by examining the disclaimer of the ad (e.g., "Paid for by . . ."). These commercials must be paid for with hard money and are disclosed to the FEC, making them much less advantageous than issue ads. Over 95 percent of commercials aired by parties and groups were issue ads.
7. In several cases, ads were broadcast in districts where CMAG markets reached as few as 35 percent of residents.
8. The top dozen races in 1998 in order of spending on issue ads were OH 6 ($664 thousand), NV 1 ($655), MI 10 ($574), UT 2 ($518), WA 3 ($427), PA 13 ($393), CT 5 ($392), NM 3 ($385), MI 8 ($380), KY 4 ($363), FL 3 ($361), and WI 1 ($310). In 2000, the twelve most expensive issue ad campaigns were in CA 49 ($5.3 million), NJ 12 ($4.1), FL 22 ($3.5), MI 8 ($3.5), CA 36 ($3.3), NJ 7 ($3.0), KY 3 ($2.8), MN 6 ($2.3), PA 4 ($1.9), NY 2 ($1.8), AR 4 ($1.8), and FL 8 ($1.7).
9. Green and I include a fifth causal variable, challenger political quality, in our model (Green and Krasno 1988, 1990). This nine point measure rates the attractiveness and political skill of the challenger and has a substantial direct effect on the vote plus interacts with challenger spending so that better challengers get more bang for their campaign buck. Unfortunately, a format change in *Congressional Quarterly* makes it impossible to collect these data for 1998 or 2000. Comparing the effects of campaign spending from 1984 to 1996 with and without challenger quality shows a relatively minor impact from its omission, though one that varies from year to year.
10. Studies routinely find that fundraising is the number one complaint of members of Congress (Jacobson 2000, Schram 1995).
11. Aspirin consumption is a useful analogy. It is easy to see that aspirin relieves headaches by gauging patients' conditions both *before* and *after* consumption. If one only observes part of the story—the number of aspirins a patient took and how they felt afterward—it would appear as if they caused headaches instead of curing them, since the patients with the worst headaches take the most aspirin.
12. By comparison, candidates in these races spent over $471 million. There was one contest (CA 49 in 2000) in which issue advertisers spent more than both candidates combined. This

was the only case in which the cost of issue ads for the incumbent ($2.6 million) exceeded incumbent Rep. Brian Bilbray's own campaign ($1.8 million). There were nine races in which issue advocacy for challengers outpaced challenger expenditures, including Bilbray's opponent Susan Davis, though several involved trivial ad buys by groups in noncompetitive elections.

13. This is a common conclusion in analyses of campaign spending, although my previous research has shown greater parity between incumbents and challenger (Green and Krasno 1988, 1990). The results of the analysis of this two-year period are within the standard errors of earlier estimates. The reason for the gap in productivity is that incumbents begin the campaign much better known than their challengers, meaning that they do not pick up the same quick gains from their first dollars spent as their opponents do.

14. This helps explain the huge discrepancy between FEC reports of parties' expenditures (using both hard and soft money) and CMAG's figures (see La Raja and Jarvis-Shean 2001).

15. The vast majority of the issue ad dollars in both years went to support opposing sets of candidates in the same districts. One can easily imagine the determination (and the fundraising appeals) at party or interest group headquarters to be sure that their side match any effort by their counterparts.

16. One piece of supporting evidence is that the addition of issue advocacy spending does very little to help improve the "fit" of the model, the amount of the variation accounted for by campaign spending, previous vote share, and the party dummy. The R^2 of the model with issue advocacy is just .001 greater (.833) than the R^2 of the model without it.

17. The two challengers who might owe their predicted victories to issue advocacy are Rep. Susan Davis (D-CA) who defeated Bilbray in 2000 and Eleanor Jordan who, despite expectations, lost to Rep. Ann Northup (R-TN) in 2000. Challengers won just 7 of the 465 races examined here and came within two percentage points in another three fairly representative of incumbents' success in 1998 and 2000.

THE IMPACT OF ISSUE ADVOCACY
AND PARTY SOFT MONEY ELECTIONEERING

DAVID B. MAGLEBY[1]

The 1996 election marked a watershed in the campaign strategies of political parties and interest groups when they dramatically expanded their use of soft money and issue advocacy to elect and defeat particular candidates. Although both soft money and issue advocacy electioneering were used before 1996, the scope and impact of the spending was unparalleled. The Clinton-Gore campaign's use of Democratic National Committee soft money to define Clinton in positive terms and set the agenda of the campaign began in the summer of 1995; the Republicans responded in kind beginning a year later.[2]

Parties were not the only players. Having endured major losses in 1994, the American Federation of Labor–Congress of Industrial Organizations (AFL-CIO) spent an estimated $35 million in 1996, targeted largely at freshmen Republicans in the House of Representatives.[3] Business groups predictably followed labor's lead, spending millions of their own in issue advocacy to defend the Republicans and attack some Democrats.[4]

Since 1996, parties and interest groups have expanded their largely unregulated soft money–funded campaigns. In the 1997–1998 election cycle, congressional campaign committees and interest groups spent more soft money on issue advocacy than they had in any previous year.[5] Given the different turnout dynamics of a midterm election, parties, and especially interest groups, broadened their communications assault to include substantial efforts on the ground through mail, telephone, and direct personal contact. Again, the AFL-CIO took the lead.[6] The expansion of noncandidate campaigning continued in 2000, with the greatest growth in party soft money coming from the Democratic campaign committees, especially the Democratic Senatorial Campaign Committee.[7]

Noncandidate campaigning has the advantage of no contribution limits; in contrast, candidate and party hard money contributions are limited. Issue advocacy can also avoid disclosing the source of the funds and how they are spent. Because this money falls outside the regulatory regime of the Federal Election Campaign Act (FECA) and the control of candidates, it is aptly labeled "outside money."

Outside money has become an important part of recent federal elections because it permits parties and interest groups to target large sums of money to the most competitive contests, which determine the control of Congress. The fact that the 1998 and 2000 election cycles had comparatively few competitive contests with so much riding on them only reinforced the desire of parties and interest groups to find ways to channel money into these races.[8]

Interest groups and national party committees decide to use issue advocacy or soft money for five reinforcing reasons. First, groups and party committees can raise money for these purposes that in some cases could not otherwise be spent on federal elections. Second, control of Congress is so tightly contested that they feel a compelling need to invest as much as possible in the most competitive races. Third, outside money provides them with a means to influence the agenda of the most visible and reported upon federal contests and, in so doing, advance their issue agenda or block an opponent's. Fourth, mounting a visible outside money campaign may reinforce a group's claim to an issue domain and encourage people to join the group. Fifth, not all groups or individuals want their identity known as they campaign. For those groups, issue advocacy permits them to campaign for or against a candidate anonymously. Examples of this in 1998 and 2000 included American Family Voices, funded largely by the American Federation of Federal, State, County, and Municipal Employees (AFSCME); Citizens for Better Medicare, funded primarily by the pharmaceutical industry; Republicans for Clean Air, funded by Texas businessman Sam Wyly; and Jane Fonda, who contributed $6.2 million to Planned Parenthood, $3 million to NARAL, $1.3 million to Voters for Choice, and $5 million to the League of Conservation Voters to fund issue advocacy.[9]

Issue ads and soft money have become critical tools in today's federal electoral system, which is ironic because technically, neither is supposed to be used for the election or defeat of federal candidates. The Supreme Court in its landmark *Buckley v. Valeo* (1976) decision distinguished between campaign speech (express advocacy), which uses words like "vote for," "vote against," "elect," or "defeat," and noncampaign speech, labeled "issue advocacy" because it does not use the magic words. The court clarifies "express terms" with footnote 52: "This construction would restrict the application of section 608 (e)(1) to communications containing express words of advocacy of election or defeat, such as 'vote for,' 'elect,' 'support,' 'cast your ballot for,' 'Smith for Congress,' 'vote against,' 'defeat,' 'reject.'"[10] According to legislation and administrative rulings, parties should use soft money (technically known as nonfederal dollars) for "party-building purposes" and should use limited and disclosed hard money (federal dollars) to campaign for and against a candidate.[11] But parties spend millions of dollars in soft money to promote and attack candidates, as do interest groups.

What are the effects of these modes of electioneering? Can outside money influence voters as effectively as regulated and controlled hard money? This chapter will focus on two important outcomes of outside money. First, we will look at how voters perceive issue advocacy. In October 2000 we conducted the first study of its kind; we showed voters different types of political ads to determine if the Supreme Court's "magic words" test is a meaningful distinction for voters. We also measured the effect of candidate, party, and different types of issue advocacy commercials on voters.

Second, we will consider outside money's effect on campaigns. How has the advent of issue advocacy and the growth in party soft money influenced the demand for hard and soft money, changed candidate, party, and interest group tactics, and altered the way groups communicate when faced with so much electioneering activity? To better understand these and related questions, we will consider evidence gathered over the last two election cycles in thirty-three congressional contests and presidential primaries in five states.[12]

Taken together, an assessment of how voters perceive noncandidate campaign communications, the extent to which these efforts persuade voters to support or oppose candidates, and how outside money influences campaigns will help address important public policy issues in campaign finance reform. For example, if the effect of soft money and election issue advocacy is indistinguishable from candidate advertising, why are these forms of communication treated differently in the law?

More broadly, the surge in noncandidate electioneering raises issues about the role of candidates, parties, and interest groups in our democracy. If candidates are no longer in charge of much of the content of the campaigns, what is the role of elections? Is party advertising built around a European-style party message, or is it merely another way to direct money into a particular race, with no consistent party emphasis? Does the enlarged role of parties and interest groups have the potential to make Congress more responsive to these forces and less responsive to their constituents?

STUDY DESIGN AND METHODOLOGY

The Supreme Court's *Buckley v. Valeo* distinction between express and issue advocacy, along with the 1979 legislation and subsequent administrative rulings permitting parties to spend soft money have encouraged multiple campaigns to communicate with the same voters in the same contest.

TWO WAVES OF RESEARCH

To determine whether these distinctions have any real consequence on the voters, we designed a multimode study of random samples of respondents. First, Wirthlin Worldwide conducted focus groups in Princeton, New Jersey, and Lansing, Michigan, on September 18–19, 2000. Both cities were ground zero in competitive House races and a total of four groups (N = 25 per group for a total of N = 100 participants) were held to explore the extent to which respondents differentiated among communications for candidate, party soft money, election issue advocacy, and pure issue advocacy.[13] All participants were registered voters who indicated they were likely to vote in the upcoming election. In the focus groups, we showed participants eight commercials, alternating the order of the commercials in each session. We also asked respondents to view samples of political mail that came from candidates, political parties, and issue advocacy groups. Although focus groups are generally limited by their small sample, in our case by one hundred, they provided insight into voters' thinking and informed the next phase of the study, a large sample Web TV survey.

Our second wave of research, a national Web TV survey of 2,035 registered voters in eleven treatment groups, used data innovatively collected by Knowledge Networks (formerly InterSurvey).[14] Commercials were downloaded into a random sample of homes, and respondents answered questions about the ads on their Web TVs. The study was in the field between October 25 and 31, 2000. Each treatment group was shown three commercials, with the order of the commercials randomized across each treatment group to combat any possible learning effect during the experiment. In the aggregate, between 734 and 910 respondents saw each of the eight ads used in the study. Every possible pairing of ads was found in at least one of the eleven treatment groups, which had samples ranging from 158 to 213.

COMMERCIALS SELECTED

The sample of commercials used for both the focus groups and the national survey was drawn from a set of commercials shown from November 1999 to early September 2000 and collected by the National Journal Group on its Hotline Political Ad tapes. Our objective was to identify typical commercials for candidate, party soft money, election issue advocacy, and pure issue advocacy. For consistency across states and over time, we selected the following commercials, all related to the presidential race or national policy issues:

> *Gore Candidate Ad (Gore):* "Bean Counter," paid for by Gore-Lieberman, Inc. In this thirty-second ad, Vice President Al Gore is shown outdoors in a denim shirt, jeans, and boots speaking to a crowd. He explains that HMO accountants should not be able to determine medical treatments, that this decision should be left to doctors. In answer to this dilemma, Gore promotes a patient's bill of rights.

Bush Candidate Ad (Bush): "Education Agenda," paid for by Bush-Cheney 2000, Inc. Speaking at a large convention, Governor George W. Bush explains the problems that face American schools today. An announcer explains that Bush's education plan includes reforming Head Start, improving reading, and restoring local control and school accountability. Bush closes by saying that now is the time to renew the promise to help America's schools.

Democratic Party Ad (DNC): "Judge," paid for by the Democratic National Committee. In ominous tones, an announcer informs viewers that George W. Bush has broken his promise to secure health care for children in Texas. The announcer cites a recent court ruling requiring Texas to take immediate corrective action. It closes with the line, "The Bush record: it's becoming an issue."

Republican Party Ad (RNC): "Really," paid for by the Republican National Committee. A television flashes different snippets of Vice President Al Gore's more questionable moments as a female voice explains the different scenes. Footage is shown of the visit to the Buddhist Temple and the interview in which Gore claimed credit for inventing the Internet. The final line: "Yeah right, and I invented the remote control. Another round of this and I'll sell my television."

Election Issue Ad (Voices): "Bush," paid for by American Family Voices. While panning through a scene that looks like the aftermath of a political convention, an announcer explains all the ways that Governor George W. Bush is beholden to special interests. Different signs indicating special interests like the insurance industry, nursing home operators, and drug companies are followed by the amounts these groups have given in donations to the Bush campaign. The voice asks viewers to "Tell Bush when special interests win, America's families lose."

Election Issue Ad (RLC): "Social Security," paid for by Republican Leadership Coalition. An older woman explains how Al Gore's Medicare drug premium will cost the public. She ends by giving this message to Al Gore: "Get your hands off my Social Security check! It's not enough now."

Pure Issue Ad (Hospitals): "Nurse," paid for by the Coalition to Protect America's Health Care. A nurse in a busy hospital explains that the budget cuts Congress and the president have made hurt hospitals. She explains that many services are being cut back and some hospitals have been forced to close. With the current surplus, the nurse implores the viewer to "Tell Washington to restore funding to our hospitals."

Pure Issue Ad (Priorities): "Nuclear Winter," paid for by Iowans for Sensible Priorities. Multiple nuclear explosions are shown and the viewer is told that the United States has more than enough nuclear weapons to protect itself. It ends by asking the viewer to "Tell the presidential candidates the Cold War is over. Invest in kids, not nuclear weapons."

We selected the above commercials because they were representative of national political ads shown during the time frame and the kind of ads run by the different groups. We also chose issue ads that did not contain the electioneering words specifically mentioned in *Buckley* to test the effects of outside money election issue advocacy ads as opposed to express advocacy ads. The candidate ads we selected also did not contain the "magic words." This choice was unintentional, but not surprising, because only 4 percent of candidate election ads actually used the magic words in 1998 and 9.6 percent in 2000.[15] For most of the campaign, especially through early September, candidate ads were generally positive, focusing on the candidate running the ad. This fact constrained our choice of candidate ads. We avoided ads that were extremely critical or controversial.

MONITORING CAMPAIGN EFFECTS

We then monitored the effects of outside-money activity by party soft money and interest groups in actual campaigns with the help of teams of academics in seventeen competitive congressional contests in 2000. These academics built reconnaissance teams throughout their states or districts to help monitor the mail, telephone, and interpersonal forms of political communication. These teams included colleagues, university or college alumni, political reporters, consultants, friends, neighbors, and a diverse set of politically connected people. In addition, we provided each academic with mailing labels of Common Cause members in their state or district. In most of our sample contests, we also had the cooperation of members of the League of Women voters, who either provided lists or communicated directly to their members.[16] BYU alumni in all of the contests were also asked to collect and send their political mail and to report personal or telephone contacts during the campaign. The scope of communications collected included not only issue advocacy and party soft money–funded advertising, but also independent expenditures and internal communications within unions, corporations, and membership organizations. Academics also visited local TV and radio stations to collect ad buy information. The research reported in the second part of this chapter has to do with the impact of outside money on campaign strategy and conduct.

THE IMPACT OF OUTSIDE MONEY ON VOTERS

Understanding how voters perceive and react to soft money and issue advocacy communications helps us address two important questions. First, do voters perceive, as the Courts and administrative agencies have, that issue advocacy that avoids the magic words is unrelated to the election? At its core, the logic of the *Buckley* express versus issue advocacy distinction is the assumption that voters perceive issue advocacy to be different than express advocacy or candidate communications. Similarly, do voters perceive differences between party communications and candidate communications in terms of any component that might be perceived as "party building"? Second, what, if any, impact do these different forms of communication have in influencing how people vote?

VOTER PERCEPTION OF ISSUE ADVOCACY AND PARTY SOFT MONEY COMMUNICATIONS

Voters see clear differences between pure issue ads, which have no candidate referent, and election issue ads. When asked, "What do you believe was the primary objective or purpose of this ad?" respondents in the national Knowledge Networks survey clearly distinguished between the issue ads that had an election focus and those that did not.[17] As expected, more than two-thirds of respondents (70 and 71 percent) saw the pure issue ads as primarily about an issue. However, less than 10 percent (6 and 8 percent) of the respondents saw the election issue advocacy ads as primarily about an issue (see Table 5.1). Instead, 80 and 81 percent of respondents said these election issue advocacy ads were urging them to vote against a candidate.[18] Similarly, respondents overwhelmingly saw party soft money ads as urging them to vote for or against a candidate, and a scant 2 percent of respondents saw either soft money ad as primarily attempting to promote the party. In fact, neither party ad even mentioned the name of the party, even though such ads are presumed to promote the party. When we aggregate the responses "vote for" and "vote against," the results are even more striking, with nearly 90 percent

TABLE 5.1   ISSUE ADVOCACY ADS

What do you believe was the *primary* objective or purpose of this ad?

	CANDIDATE ADS		PARTY ADS		ELECTION ISSUE ADS		PURE ISSUE ADS	
	GORE	BUSH	DNC	RNC	VOICES	RLC	HOSPITALS	PRIORITIES
Persuade you to vote for a candidate	62%	72%	7%	7%	8%	8%	6%	7%
Persuade you to vote against a candidate	2	2	79	82	81	80	6	6
Present issue	30	20	11	5	6	8	71	70
Persuade you to get out and vote	1	1	1	—	1	1	4	5
Promote a particular political party	2	2	2	2	2	1	4	4
Raise money	—	—	—	—	—	—	5	—
Other	1	1	—	1	1	—	1	1
Not sure	1	2	1	2	1	1	3	8
Number of respondents	750	744	707	783	718	900	727	777

of the respondents viewing the election issue advocacy ads and the party soft money ads as primarily urging them to vote for or against a candidate.[19]

Further evidence that the magic words distinction is not meaningful to respondents is data from the following question: "On a scale of 1 to 7, with 1 meaning the ad was *not at all intended* to influence how you vote in the presidential election, and 7 meaning the ad was *clearly intended* to influence how you vote in the presidential election, how would you rank this ad?"

A remarkable 70 to 71 percent scored the election issue advocacy ads as "7," and 83 percent gave the ads a 6 or a 7. Party soft money ads received the same level of responses, with 82 to 83 percent receiving a 6 or a 7. In contrast, less than one-fifth of respondents gave the pure issue ads a 7, and less than one-third gave them a 6 or 7. The differences in the means for each ad, listed in Table 5.2, further reinforce the finding that respondents saw party soft money ads and election issue advocacy ads as attempts to influence their vote. In fact, all four ads in question scored a 6.3 mean out of the maximum of seven. Interestingly, the candidate ads scored significantly lower means (5.7 and 5.9) than the party soft money and election issue advocacy ads. Using this different measurement tool, we find that respondents rank the party and election issue ads as the most clearly intended to affect their vote.

The focus groups provided us the possibility to further test these issues beyond the medium of television. In the focus groups we provided each participant with a sample of political mail representing the same categories of sponsorship as the television advertisements: candidate, party, and the two

TABLE 5.2   SOFT MONEY ADS

On a scale of 1 to 7, with 1 meaning the ad was *not at all intended* to influence your vote for or against a presidential candidate, and 7 meaning the ad was *clearly intended* to influence your vote for or against a presidential candidate, how would you rank this ad?

	CANDIDATE ADS		PARTY ADS		ELECTION ISSUE ADS		PURE ISSUE ADS	
	GORE	*BUSH*	*DNC*	*RNC*	*VOICES*	*RLC*	*HOSPITALS*	*PRIORITIES*
1	5%	3%	3%	2%	3%	2%	24%	27%
2	3	1	1	—	—	1	8	8
3	3	4	1	2	2	1	13	10
4	11	10	5	6	5	5	18	20
5	11	11	7	7	6	8	13	11
6	14	13	13	11	12	13	5	6
7	52	58	70	71	71	70	19	16
Mean	5.7	5.9	6.3	6.3	6.3	6.3	3.8	3.6
Number of respondents	750	744	707	783	718	900	727	777

types of issue advocacy. In our 1998 study of competitive federal elections, we learned that mail was an important element of campaign communications.[20] Pure issue mail, or mail from interest groups that did not have a campaign theme or message, was seen by 78 percent of the respondents as about an issue, and only 7 percent about urging voters to vote for or against a candidate. Voters perceive communications funded by outside money as trying to persuade them to vote for or against a candidate and not as communications unrelated to the voting choice.

IMPACT ON VOTE INTENTION

Does party and interest group election issue advocacy influence voters? Before showing the Web TV survey respondents any of the commercials, we asked them for their voting intentions.[21] Consistent with other national surveys taken at the time, our survey found Gore ahead 47 percent to 43 percent. Not surprisingly, given the timing of the survey, only 3 percent of respondents were undecided. Nader had the support of 5 percent and Pat Buchanan 1 percent in the survey. In subsequent analyses we will only examine the Bush, Gore, Nader, and undecided voters.

After viewing each commercial, respondents were asked, "Did this ad make you more likely or less likely to vote for George W. Bush?" The same question was repeated for Al Gore. Respondents were also given the option of answering, "It had no effect on my vote," and "Not sure." Table 5.3 presents the impact of all eight ads on Bush voters, Gore voters, Nader voters and undecided voters. The ads are categorized by the intended beneficiary (Gore allies, Bush allies, and pure issue) and then further ordered according to the ad's sponsor (candidate, party, and interest group). It is important to note the small number of cases for both Nader and undecided voters.[22]

With few exceptions, the most frequent response for all eight TV ads was "It had no effect on my vote," ranging from 41 to 91 percent. However, a distinct difference is found between pure issue ads and outside money election issue ads by parties and interest groups. On average, 78 percent of respondents said the pure issue ads had "no effect" on their vote intention, while only 42 percent of respondents answered "no effect" for party soft money ads and interest group election issue advocacy. This strongly demonstrates the divide between pure issue ads and outside money ads on vote intention.

The candidate, party soft money, and interest group ads generally reinforced the respondents' vote intentions. For instance, 52 percent of the Gore voters were more likely to vote for Gore after viewing the DNC ad. However, the Democratic allied ads in each instance engendered a higher rate of reinforcement for Gore than did the Republican allied ads for Bush. For example, 57 percent of Gore voters said the Gore ad made them more likely to vote for Gore, compared to 47 percent of the Bush voters who said the Bush ad made them more likely to vote for Bush. The same differential held true for the party

TABLE 5.3 EFFECT ON THE VOTE

Ads	Did this ad make you more or less likely to vote for Bush?				Did this ad make you more or less likely to vote for Gore?			
	More	Less	No Effect	N	More	Less	No Effect	N
Bush Voters								
Gore Allies								
Gore	21%	3%	73%	326	7%	20%	67%	326
DNC (pty)	22	8	66	298	4	34	58	298
Voices (ig)	18	6	71	331	5	27	67	331
Bush Allies								
Bush	47	1	51	326	1	30	67	326
RNC (pty)	40	2	56	332	1	41	55	332
RLC (ig)	40	1	56	409	1	43	55	409
Pure Issue								
Hospitals	16	0	80	294	0	15	80	294
Priorities	12	0.3	83	327	0	12	84	327
Gore Voters								
Gore Allies								
Gore	4%	37%	55%	356	57%	1%	41%	356
DNC (pty)	2	54	43	325	52	2	43	325
Voices (ig)	1	52	45	329	50	2	45	329
Bush Allies								
Bush	5	23	69	342	23	2	72	342
RNC (pty)	3	37	57	350	26	4	67	350
RLC (ig)	5	26	63	418	18	10	66	418
Pure Issue								
Hospitals	2	14	78	357	13	2	79	357
Priorities	0.3	17	73	346	16	0.3	76	346
Nader Voters								
Gore Allies								
Gore	8%	16%	71%	38	29%	11%	55%	38
DNC (pty)	0	43	57	44	16	11	71	44
Voices (ig)	0	45	48	29	24	3	66	29
Bush Allies								
Bush	8	13	75	40	3	15	80	40
RNC (pty)	5	28	63	43	5	26	61	43
RLC (ig)	10	15	68	41	5	24	63	41
Pure Issue								
Hospitals	8	15	70	40	8	13	70	40
Priorities	3	3	91	34	0	6	91	34
Undecided Voters								
Gore Allies								
Gore	6%	6%	53%	17	6%	6%	53%	17
DNC (pty)	0	24	47	17	18	0	53	17
Voices (ig)	0	23	32	22	9	0	41	22
Bush Allies								
Bush	6	6	61	18	6	6	56	18
RNC (pty)	4	4	50	26	0	15	54	26
RLC (ig)	5	0	73	22	0	9	59	22
Pure Issue								
Hospitals	0	9	73	22	5	0	58	22
Priorities	0	0	80	15	0	0	80	15

ads, with the DNC at 52 percent and the RNC at 40 percent. Likewise, the Democratic party ad resulted in a 50 percent "more likely to vote for Gore" response among Gore voters, compared to the Republican party ad's 40 percent "more likely to vote for Bush" response among Bush voters. The same tendency was evident when we examined the impact of ads on different categories of party identification. A variety of reasons may have caused this consistent 10 to 12 percent differential: Gore voters may have known less about George W. Bush and, after exposure to the ads against Bush, became more committed to Gore; Bush voters may have been more aware of Vice President Gore's negatives before exposure to the ads and therefore may have been less influenced by the Bush allied ads; or, Gore voters may have been less sure of their support for the vice president, but, after exposure to the Gore allied ads, they felt more inclined to support him.

Interestingly, the highest percentage of reinforcement tended to be among Republican defectors. After watching the Gore commercial, 70 percent of the Republican Gore supporters were more likely to vote for Gore, compared to 58 percent of the Democratic Gore supporters. Similarly, after viewing the DNC ad, 59 percent of the Republican Gore supporters were more likely to vote for Gore, compared to 55 percent of the Democratic Gore supporters. The same phenomenon, however, did not exist among Bush supporters. Although a certain percentage of Democratic Bush supporters were more likely to vote for Bush after seeing Bush allied ads, a higher percentage existed among Republican Bush supporters.

The sample of ads we showed voters did not persuade them to be more likely to vote for a candidate they originally opposed. Among Gore and Bush voters, not once did even 10 percent of the voters say that they were more likely to vote for the opposing candidate after seeing ads for the opposing candidate. In fact, the evidence presented in Table 5.3 (on page 93) reveals that ads attacking a candidate cause about one in five voters who favor the candidate being attacked to be more inclined to support that candidate, in essence reinforcing the opposition's vote. Take for example the Republican party ad that charged Gore with constantly reinventing himself and showed footage of him raising illegal contributions at a Buddhist temple in 1996. After seeing the ad, 26 percent of the Gore voters said they were more likely to vote for Gore; in essence, the Republican-backed ad backfired by further reinforcing the opposition vote. The same reinforcement occurred with Democratic ads, as 22 percent of the Bush voters said they were more likely to vote for Bush after seeing the Democratic party ad.

When campaign communications are broadcast, as with these ads, advertisers risk activating as many opponents as supporters. This is one reason why parties and groups have increasingly turned to more targeted communications like telephone, radio, and mail. In the next section, we will further investigate how outside money has affected campaigns by investing in the more targeted forms of communications.

The candidate communications in our sample of ads were positive presentations of each candidate, a contrast to the party and election issue ads that criticized the opposing candidate. Do these negative ads have the effect of making voters less likely to support their preferred candidate? Only 4 percent of Gore voters reported being less inclined to vote for Gore after seeing the GOP attack on Gore; twice as many Bush voters, 8 percent, were less likely to vote for Bush after seeing the Democratic attack on Bush. These small differences reinforce the earlier finding that Democrats (candidate, party, and allied group) had a consistent advantage in motivating people to be more likely to vote for Gore.

In 2000, major party candidates, their allied groups, and their parties faced an additional challenge in trying to persuade Nader supporters to defect. Table 5.3 (on page 93) shows the effects of the various ads on the Nader voters, an analysis limited by the small proportion of Nader voters in the sample.[23] The Gore allied ads appeared to be more effective at persuading the Nader voters to vote for Gore than were the Bush ads in persuading them to vote for Bush. Much of this may be explained by the fact that only 13 percent of Nader voters within the sample were Republicans. Therefore, the Gore allied ads presumably played to a more receptive audience. Additionally, the Nader voters tended to see the ads as having no effect on their vote for Gore or Bush at a higher rate than the Gore or Bush voters.

THE IMPACT OF OUTSIDE MONEY ON CAMPAIGNS

To assess the role of outside money on campaigns, we recruited academics from states and districts to monitor the full range of campaign communications by candidates, parties, and interest groups. We also collected mail, recorded telephone calls and instances of personal contacts, and conducted scores of interviews with party and interest group operatives. Through this type of groundwork, we found that outside money affects both campaign strategy and campaign agendas. Outside money forces candidate campaigns to anticipate and deal with a wider range of issues and possible opposition attacks. Outside money also alters the timing of campaigns because outside groups enter the game early and force candidates to raise more money and spend it earlier. The basic campaign lesson is to raise as much money as possible in anticipation of the need to counter the opposing team. In short, competitive campaigns are no longer dominated by candidate strategies.

IMPACT ON CAMPAIGN STRATEGY

Arguably, one of the most visible and important consequences of outside money in competitive races is the approximate doubling of campaign costs, particularly with the volume of television and radio advertising.[24] In several races that we monitored in 1998 and 2000, the availability of broadcast advertising time was scarce. Candidates, parties, and interest groups had learned the strategic impact of the high volume of television and radio advertising in competitive congressional contests. All participants have shown a tendency to lock in advertising time early for the last weeks of the campaign, before prices escalate and when they have more discretion as to when ads will run. Candidates increasingly buy nonpreemptable time, passing up their option of purchasing time at the lowest unit rate for that segment of the day. Those who wait until later in the election cycle to purchase advertising time pay a premium, sometimes double or more than double the prevailing rate. We found evidence in 2000 of a growing use of cable TV advertising, especially among the Democrats.

Also important has been the surge in expenditures on targeted mail and telephone communications. A leader in the application of these targeted tools is organized labor. The AFL-CIO shifted from a primarily broadcast approach in 1996 to a strategy more reliant on personal contact, mail, and telephone mobilization in 1998. Early in 1998, labor was under attack in California and elsewhere with paycheck protection ballot initiatives. Partly in response to these measures, labor launched a major effort to reactivate its membership, making personal contacts with each union household and reinforcing these contacts with direct mail messages.[25] This strategy of paycheck protection, initially used in California in June 1998, was used in the Nevada Senate race in 1998 to help reelect Harry Reid. In this contest about forty thousand union households were contacted in person, and each household was contacted three more times by phone, mail, or another personal visit.[26] In 2000, labor carried this strategy to the New Hampshire primary and the Iowa caucuses. In New Hampshire, labor planned seven contacts; members received phone calls, visits, and mail. The mail included a videotaped endorsement of Al Gore by AFL-CIO president John Sweeney.[27] In the Iowa caucuses, each union household in the state also received the Sweeney-Gore video tape.[28] Art Sanders and David Redlawsk, who monitored issue advocacy in the Iowa Caucuses in 2000, concluded, "The big winner . . . was labor, whose organizational efforts in the ground war were essential to Gore's victory."[29]

In the 2000 general election, labor, among other groups, appeared to follow a more nuanced strategy of communicating with a mass audience by contributing large amounts of soft money to the party campaign committees and by again implementing the 1998 grassroots strategy. Labor efforts in Michigan were substantial, not only for Al Gore in the presidential race, but also for Debbie Stabenow in the U.S. Senate race and in selected House races. Political scientist Michael Traugott, who monitored the Michigan Senate race, concluded that outside groups "may have made the difference" for Stabenow in a very tight Senate race.[30] Delaware Democrat Tom Carper is another candidate who benefited from the effects of the DNC and allied groups' energizing his Democratic base vote.[31]

Another group that deployed a well-organized voter identification and mobilization effort was the National Education Association (NEA). These kinds of grassroots organizing—voter identification and mobilization—also occurred among Republican-allied groups. For example, in 2000, the National Rifle Association (NRA) "did more and spent more than in 1996 and 1998 combined."[32] Because their main focus was to mobilize voters, they pushed absentee voting, ran ads with specific endorsements in several NRA-related magazines, and mounted a large-scale targeted mail operation, all in addition to radio and TV ads.

Communicating with voters through the mail was one of the most frequently observed strategies used by interest groups and political parties in 1998 and 2000. In our 1998 study, direct mail made up at least one-third of all campaign contacts in our sample races.[33] In 2000, voters were deluged with mail, especially in the last few weeks of the election cycle. For example, in Washington, the National Abortion and Reproductive Rights Action League (NARAL) sent four to seven mailings to about 150,000 people.[34] In the last week of the election cycle, some Washingtonians received over twelve pieces of mail per day.[35] Because of the massive amounts of mail, candidate and outside money campaigns used bold colors, oversized formats, and catchier wording to catch voters' attention. The National Federation of Independent Businesses (NFIB), for example, chose black and gold as their main colors so that voters would be able to pick NFIB mailers out of the many of red, white, and blue mailers. The League of Conservation Voters in the California Twenty-Seventh District race used a pop-up mail piece that opened much like a children's book to show the impact of urban sprawl.[36]

IMPACT ON AGENDA SETTING

Outside money can provide groups and parties with a means to influence the agenda of the most visible federal contests, and, in so doing, they may advance their issue agenda or block an opponent's.[37] For example, early in the Montana Senate primary, the Trial Lawyers attacked Republican incumbent Conrad Burns for his votes on asbestos found in vermiculite mined in Libby, Montana. They chastised Burns for cosponsoring legislation that limited corporate liability for the 375 cases of asbestos-caused illness and for the deaths of 192 people. The Trial Lawyers set the stage for Burns' Democratic challenger, Brian Schweitzer. Schweitzer picked up on the Trial Lawyer agenda and used the asbestos allegation in his campaign.[38] Citizens for Better Medicare (CBM) also helped set the agenda in Montana with ads criticizing Schweitzer's stand on prescription drugs. This time, Schweitzer was hurt by the new agenda; he was forced to spend $65,000 to counter their attacks when he only had $100,000 in his coffer.[39] Similarly, in Michigan, anti-immigration groups attacked Senator Spencer Abraham (R). These attacks caught Abraham off guard and forced him to spend money early.[40]

THE SURROGATE CAMPAIGN

Outside money is a team sport, and the two parties have mastered ways of telegraphing to their allies the targets as well as the themes of their messages. Although there is no evidence of formal coordination or collusion, the relatively few competitive contests and the public nature of this activity makes the strategy of all participants relatively transparent.

Outside money can therefore be tremendously beneficial to candidates because it acts as a surrogate campaign, providing extra advertising support to a candidate when the candidate lacks the resources to communicate themselves. Debbie Stabenow experienced this in her 2000 Senate race; unable to afford broadcast ads in the summer, her party and allied groups stepped in and ran ads supporting her. Because of this help, Stabenow was able to conserve her resources.[41] The Democratic party played a similar role in Chuck Robb's 2000 Virginia Senate race, spending over $9 million in hard and soft money.[42]

Candidates do not always accept the offered help from outside groups, sometimes much to their disadvantage. One candidate who likely regrets turning down party help is Delaware senator William Roth, who on the advice of his manager, declined assistance from the National Republican Senatorial Commission (NRSC) because they didn't think Delawareans would like the new, more negative campaign strategy of outside groups.[43] Overall party spending in the Delaware Senate race was $4,974,199 for the Democrats and $841,954 for the Republicans.[44] The business community then perceived that the Roth campaign did not want issue advocacy support, and so they were less involved than in other races, which was ironic given Roth's position as chair of the Senate Finance Committee.

The more typical pattern is for candidates to try and exploit an outside endorsement of themselves or an attack on their opponent by stressing their own positives on the same set of issues, an obvious contrast if their opponent is under attack in that issue dimension. Roth's opponent, Tom Carper, welcomed Democratic party soft money ads. Because the Democratic ads covered generic issues like health care and Social Security and attacked Roth's voting record on each of these issues, Carper was free to run a more positive campaign that focused on more specific issues raised by the Roth campaign.[45]

CANDIDATE ACCOUNTABILITY

Although candidates sometimes succeed in taking the high road and leaving the negative advertising to the outside groups, such attempts often backfire. Voters often are unable distinguish who was behind the advertisement they saw or mail they received. In the national survey, we found that respondents were often confused as to whether party ads were paid for by candidates or parties. More than 40 percent of the time, the respondents thought the party ads were paid for by a candidate.[46] In contrast, when we asked focus group respondents who they thought paid for the four types of political mail (candidate, party, election issue, and pure issue), three-quarters of respondents in the focus groups correctly identified an interest group as the organization that paid for pure issue advocacy mail. Voters therefore often mistakenly believe the negative advertising done by outside groups is actually done by the candidate campaigns. Even when voters correctly identified the parties as sponsors of the ads, our survey showed that a vast majority (90 percent) hold the candidates responsible to a "great degree" or to "some degree."

Given the voters' perception of candidate responsibility, candidates face the reality that outside money spent presumably for their benefit may actually hurt them in the race. The often more negative tone in campaigns that comes as a result of outside money gets blamed on the candidates. In the 1998 Utah Second Congressional District race, challenger Lily Eskelson (D) described outside money as a double-edged sword: It was helpful to have a group thank her and attack her opponent, but that group's actions were "out of control of the candidates."[47] Eskelsen was aided by a group called Americans for Limited Terms. These ads were mostly anti-Cook, Eskelsen's Republican opponent. According to a KBYU–Utah Colleges Exit Poll, 47 percent of those polled thought that the Utah Second Congressional District race was more negative than recent House races. Of that 47 percent, 74 percent blamed the candidates for the negativity, 15 percent blamed the parties, and 8 percent blamed interest groups.[48] Similarly, toward the end of the 2000 Montana Senate race, both candidates commented on the negativity that prevailed because of party and interest group involvement: "It's so negative, it's unbelievable . . . We're not building a state; we're tearing it down," said Burns. Schweitzer agreed, saying, "It's the ugliest race in America."[49]

When parties or allied groups exaggerate or make mistakes in their campaign communications, it is the candidates who are asked to defend or disavow the communication. In Kentucky 6 and New Jersey 12 in 2000, the DCCC had to pull ads because of inaccuracies. The Democratic candidates then became the target of charges of inaccuracy and, in the case of Scotty Baesler, lying.[50] Some candidates, like Bob Inglis (R) in the 1998 South Carolina Senate election, may even criticize the tone and content of their own party ads.[51]

ALLOCATING OUTSIDE MONEY

Another consequence of the growing importance of outside money is the enlarged power of those who decide where it will be allocated. Parties and interest groups that play the outside money game invest heavily in polling and campaign consultants to advise them on their best investment opportunities. Once poll results are in, the allocation process can frustrate some candidates, as was the case in 1998 when Linda Smith expressed frustration that NRSC soft money was flowing to Wisconsin to assist Mark Neumann (R) in challenging Democratic incumbent Russ Feingold. Smith asserted that the allocation process had more to do with the campaign finance reform issue positions of the respective candidates than their respective standing in the polls. Kentucky Senator Mitch McConnell, NRSC chair, was the leading Senate opponent of campaign finance reform. Smith favored campaign finance reform, Neumann did not, and Feingold was cosponsor with John McCain of the McCain-Feingold campaign finance reform legislation. Dave Hansen, political director of the NRSC in 1998, insisted the campaign finance reform issue had nothing to do with the allocation decision; rather, the money went to Wisconsin because Neumann had better numbers.[52]

Interest group issue advocacy campaigns also often allocate their money based on independent tracking polls. Among the groups that did independent polling in 2000 were the NEA, AFL-CIO, Trial Lawyers, NAACP, NRA, Chamber of Commerce, and all four congressional campaign committees. Interest groups have similar criteria for issue advocacy or independent expenditure designation, including the candidate's "fit" with core issues of concern to the group.

OUTSIDE MONEY IN NOMINATION BATTLES

The relative scarcity of competitive contests and the high stakes each has for control of Congress has meant that parties and interest groups occasionally invest outside money in nomination battles in hopes that the most electable candidate will be nominated. In 2000, for example, the DCCC backed the losing candidate in the primary in Pennsylvania's Fourth District.[53] Interest groups that pursue a similar strategy sometimes have to regroup quickly if their preferred candidate fails to win the nomination, as evidenced in Oklahoma 2; organized labor backed Bill Settle, who lost the primary, but quickly supported Carson in the general election.[54]

CONCLUSION

The increase in outside money since 1996 has substantially affected both the electorate and campaigns in competitive contests. Outside money has increased the lack of control candidates have on campaigns by setting issue agendas, running sometimes damaging negative campaigns, and driving up the cost of these campaigns. Candidates have also benefited from outside money to bolster their own base, especially when they lack funds. Outside money has therefore made elections a team sport.

The allocation of money into relatively few competitive races now results in millions of dollars in expenditures in a single House and Senate race, thereby altering campaign dynamics in fundamental ways. Outside money increases the amount of money candidates must raise to be competitive and prepared to respond to the opposing team. It motivates parties and congressional leadership to put a premium on raising and spending soft money because the absence of limits on soft money expenditures permits parties to defend candidates from assaults by the opposing team. Finally, interest groups also see strategic advantages to investing not only in the conventional ways by giving heavily to incumbents, leadership PACs, and parties, as controlled and limited under FECA, but also to investing selectively and on a large scale in the contests that will determine congressional control. All of this fosters an arms race kind of mentality; candidates don't know how much they will need to spend, so they start early and raise as much as possible. It is also clear that contributors understand the dynamic of this new world of campaign finance and are willing to max out in hard dollars and give generously in soft dollars to interest groups as they choose.

But has the increase in outside money been ultimately worth it? More than swaying voters, outside money works to reinforce the vote. However, in close elections like those we monitored in 1998 and 2000, even small percentages of voters influenced, along with the increased mobilization that has occurred with outside money, can swing an election. Enduring concerns with outside money include the lack of disclosure about the amount spent and the unknown sources funding issue ads. Not knowing who is funding an ad makes the task of evaluating it more difficult for voters. Voters' assumptions that all campaign ads come through candidates means candidates may be hurt as well as helped by outside money. The surge in campaign communications, especially the saturation ads on TV and radio, the large volume of mail, and the high number of phone calls appears to turn off voters and makes the task of reaching and motivating them more difficult. Finally, the absence of limits on outside money has led to dramatic increases in spending by all participants, reinforcing the importance of money in politics.

NOTES

1. A team of superb research associates helped me prepare and write this chapter. Anna Nibley Baker, Jason Beal, Michelle Reed, and Eric Smith helped manage the project, assisted the academics in the seventeen congressional contests, managed the database, and managed the production of three research monographs and this paper. Anna Nibley Baker, Jason Beal, and Eric Smith also assisted with the focus group and Web TV survey data collection and analysis. Nate Moses helped construct the secure Web site and assisted in its management. Kelly Patterson and Jay Goodliffe provided helpful comments on this paper. Catherine Matthews Pavia provided editorial comment on this overview section. Throughout the project we benefited from the assistance of scores of people in collecting mail and monitoring phones, in giving us time for interviews, and in consulting with us on the selection of our sample races.

2. Dick Morris, *Behind the Oval Office: Getting Reelected against All Odds* (Los Angeles: Renaissance Books, 1999), 139; and, Joe Wesley and Clyde Wilcox, "Financing the 1996 Presidential Nominations: The Last Regulated Campaign?" in *Financing the 1996 Election,* ed. John C. Green (Armonk, NY: M. E. Sharpe, 1999), 50–54.

3. Diana Dwyre, "Interest Groups and Issue Advocacy in 1996," in *Financing the 1996 Election,* ed. John C. Green (Armonk, NY: M. E. Sharpe, 1999), 203.

4. Ibid., p. 204.

5. David B. Magleby, *Outside Money: Soft Money and Issue Advocacy in the 1998 Congressional Elections* (Boulder, CO: Rowman and Littlefield, 2000).

6. Ibid.

7. David B. Magleby, ed., *Election Advocacy: Soft Money and Issue Advocacy in the 2000 Congressional Elections* Report presented at the National Press Club, Washington, D.C., February 2001, and also found at <www.byu.edu/outsidemoney>. This report will be published this year by Rowman and Littlefield.

8. For discussion of the impact of a few competitive races, see Magleby, *Outside Money: Soft Money and Issue Advocacy in the 1998 Congressional Elections;* and Magleby, ed., *Election Advocacy: Soft Money and Issue Advocacy in the 2000 Congressional Elections.*

9. Marianne Holt, "Stealth PACs Revealed: Interest Groups in the 2000 Election Overview," *The Public I*, at <www.publici.org>, April 6, 2001.

10. *Buckley v. Valeo,* 424 U.S. 1 (1976), footnote 52.

11. For further discussion of party soft money, see Frank J. Sorauf, *Money in American Elections* (Boston: Scott, Foresman and Company, 1988), 320–327.

12. 1998 Sample: CT 5, ID 2, IL 17, IA 3, KS 3, KY 6, NM 3, OH 6, OR 1, PA 13, UT 2, WI 1, KY Senate, NV Senate, NC Senate, SC Senate. 2000 Primary Sample: CA, IA, MO, NH, SC. 2000 General Election Sample: AR 4 CA 27, CT 5, IL 10, KY 6, MI 8, MT AL, NJ 12, OK 2, PA 13, PA 4, WA 2, DE Senate, MI Senate, MO Senate, MT Senate, VA Senate.

13. For the Wirthlin Worldwide methodology, please refer to Appendix D of David B. Magleby, "Dictum Without Data: The Myth of Issue Advocacy and Party Building." Report presented at the National Press Club in Washington, D.C., November 2000, also found at <www.byu.edu/outsidemoney>.

14. For the Knowledge Networks methodology, please refer to Appendix D of Magleby, "Dictum Without Data."

15. Jonathan S. Krasno and Daniel E. Seltz, *Buying Time: Television Advertising in the 1998 Congressional Elections* (New York: Brennan Center for Justice at NYU School of Law), p. 14; and "$100 Million in Sham Issue Ads Escaped Disclosure Laws in 2000," Brennan Center for Justice, 14 March 2001. At <http://www.brennancenter.org/presscenter/pressrelease_2001_0314cmag.html>, April 13, 2001.

16. We acknowledge the assistance of Ed Davis and his assistant at Common Cause, and Lloyd Leonard and Betsy Lawson at the League of Women Voters.

17. Initial statistical tests find significant differences in how respondents in the focus groups and national survey treatment groups saw pure issue ads versus election issue ads in terms of the primary purpose and intent of the ad.

18. More than three out of four (77 percent and 85 percent) focus group respondents saw the pure issue ads as having the primary objective or purpose of presenting an issue. Furthermore, 91 and 94 percent saw the election issue ads as primarily urging them to vote for or against a candidate (see Table A1, Appendix A in Magleby, "Dictum Without Data").

19. We also conducted focus groups on the same subject. Because the focus group has a small N and because the focus group results mirror the national survey results, we will not report them in this paper. Please see Magleby, "Dictum Without Data."

20. David B. Magleby, *Outside Money: Soft Money and Issue Advocacy in the 1998 Congressional Elections,* 63–76.

21. The intended vote question was worded as follows: Who are you going to vote for president in the upcoming 2000 elections? A. George W. Bush, B. Al Gore, C. Pat Buchanan, D. Ralph Nader, E. Don't Know, F. Other specify: ____; G. Will not vote.

22. We do not provide statistical tests of significance, in part because standard analysis of variance measures are not appropriate for a design like this in which different voters saw different sets of commercials. We are exploring alternative statistical tests that we intend to report in future papers.

23. An assessment of the impact of ads on undecided voters is limited by the small number of undecided voters in the sample, only 3 percent. It appears that both the Democratic and Republican ads succeeded in influencing the undecideds to be less likely to vote for the opponent. However, as was seen earlier, the Democratic ads seemed to be more successful in making the undecideds more likely to vote for their candidate.

24. Alliance for Better Campaigns, *Gouging Democracy: How the Television Industry Profiteered on Campaign 2000* (Washington, D.C.: Alliance for Better Campaigns, March 2001).

25. David B. Magleby and Kelly D. Patterson, "Campaign Consultants and Direct Democracy: Politics of Citizen Control," in *Campaign Warriors: The Role of Political Consultants in Elections*, ed. James E. Thurber and Candice J. Nelson (Washington, D.C.: Brookings Institution Press, 2000), 133–152, 202–207.
26. Tim Fakler, et al., "The 1998 Nevada Senate Race," in *Outside Money: Soft Money and Issue Advocacy in the 1998 Congressional Elections*, ed. David B. Magleby (Boulder, CO: Rowman and Littlefield, 2000).
27. Linda Fowler, Constantine Spiliotes, and Lynn Vavreck, "The Role of Issue Advocacy Groups in the New Hampshire Primary," in *Getting Inside the Outside Campaign: Issue Advocacy in the 2000 Presidential Primaries*, ed. David B. Magleby. Report presented at the National Press Club, Washington, D.C., July 2000, 30.
28. Arthur Sanders and David Redlawsk, "Money and the Iowa Caucuses," in *Getting Inside the Outside Campaign: Issue Advocacy in the 2000 Presidential Primaries*, ed. David B. Magleby. Report presented at the National Press Club, Washington, D.C., July 2000, 23.
29. Ibid., p. 27.
30. Michael Traugott, "The 2000 Michigan Senate Race," in *Election Advocacy: Soft Money and Issue Advocacy in the 2000 Congressional Elections*, ed. David B. Magleby. Report presented at the National Press Club, Washington, D.C., February 2001, 67.
31. Joseph Pika, "The 2000 Delaware Senate Race," in *Election Advocacy: Soft Money and Issue Advocacy in the 2000 Congressional Elections*, ed. David B. Magleby. Report presented at the National Press Club, Washington, D.C., February 2001, 58.
32. Glen Caroline, interview by author, November 15, 2000, Washington, D.C.
33. Magleby, *Outside Money: Soft Money and Issue Advocacy in the 1998 Congressional Elections*, 67.
34. Todd Donovan and Charles Morrow, "The 2000 Washington Second Congressional District Race," in *Election Advocacy: Soft Money and Issue Advocacy in the 2000 Congressional Elections*, ed. David B. Magleby. Report presented at the National Press Club, Washington, D.C., February 2001, 267.
35. Ibid., p. 268.
36. Magleby, *Election Advocacy: Soft Money and Issue Advocacy in the 2000 Congressional Elections*, 3.
37. Mounting a visible outside money campaign may reinforce the group's claim to an issue domain and encourage people to join the group.
38. Craig Wilson, "The 2000 Montana Senate Race," in *Election Advocacy: Soft Money and Issue Advocacy in the 2000 Congressional Elections*, ed. David B. Magleby. Report presented at the National Press Club, Washington, D.C., February 2001, 93–94.
39. Ibid., p. 99.
40. Traugott, "The 2000 Michigan Senate Race," 69.
41. Ibid., p. 62.
42. Bob Dudley, Harry Wilson, Robert Holsworth, Scott Keeter, and Steven Medvic, "The 2000 Virginia Senate Race," in *Election Advocacy: Soft Money and Issue Advocacy in the 2000 Congressional Elections*, ed. David B. Magleby. Report presented at the National Press Club, Washington, D.C., February 2001, 107.
43. Pika, "The 2000 Delaware Senate Race," 58.
44. Ibid., p. 54. See table on page 54.
45. Ibid., p. 56.
46. During the focus group discussions, 75 percent of focus group respondents said that candidate and party soft money ads are indistinguishable.
47. Jay Goodliffe, "The 1998 Utah Second Congressional District Race," in *Outside Money: Soft Money and Issue Advocacy in the 1998 Congressional Elections*, ed. David B. Magleby (Boulder, CO: Rowman and Littlefield, 2000), 180–181.
48. Goodliffe, "The 1998 Utah Second Congressional District Race," 181.
49. Craig Wilson, "The 2000 Montana Senate Race," 94–95.
50. Denny M. Miller and Donald A. Gross, "The 2000 Kentucky Sixth Congressional District Race," 177; and Adam J. Berinsky and Susan S. Lederman, "The 2000 New Jersey Twelfth Congressional District Race," 217–218.
51. Bill Moore and Danielle Vinson, "The 1998 South Carolina Senate Race," in *Outside Money: Soft Money and Issue Advocacy in the 1998 Congressional Elections*, ed. David B. Magleby (Boulder, CO: Rowman and Littlefield, 2000), 65.
52. Quoted in David B. Magleby, *Outside Money: Soft Money and Issue Advocacy in the 1998 Congressional Elections*, 218.

53. Christopher Jan Carman and David C. Barker, "The 2000 Pennsylvania Fourth Congressional District Race," in *Election Advocacy: Soft Money and Issue Advocacy in the 2000 Congressional Elections,* ed. David B. Magleby. Report presented at the National Press Club, Washington, D.C., February 2001, 240.

54. Rebekah Herrick and Charlie Peaden, "The 2000 Oklahoma Second Congressional District Race," in *Election Advocacy: Soft Money and Issue Advocacy in the 2000 Congressional Elections,* ed. David B. Magleby. Report presented at the National Press Club, Washington, D.C., February 2001, 228, 232.

THE VIEW FROM THE AIR

TELEVISION ADVERTISING
IN VIRGINIA'S 2000 SENATE CAMPAIGN

PAUL FREEDMAN AND L. DALE LAWTON[1]

American elections have always been hard-fought battles between determined combatants set on victory. In recent years, however, concern has grown over the tenor of political discourse and the tone of election campaigns. Scholars and citizens alike have become increasingly uneasy, as campaign attacks seem to have become commonplace—particularly attacks in campaign television advertising. Important questions have been raised about the implications of campaign quality for the quality of our democracy. In particular, some have argued that negative television ads serve to diminish feelings of political efficacy and thereby dampen voter turnout (Ansolabehere et al. 1994, 1999; Ansolabehere and Iyengar 1995). Others, however, have suggested that exposure to negative ads, far from demobilizing the electorate, may actually stimulate electoral participation (Finkel and Geer 1998; Freedman and Goldstein 1999; see also Lau et al. 1999). Such seemingly contradictory findings highlight the need for additional research, new approaches, and new lines of inquiry.

In this chapter we introduce one such new line of inquiry. We argue that the lack of consistency in findings may stem in part from a miscast conceptual approach. We suggest that the most common definitions of "negative advertising" may be too broad to capture important distinctions among campaign ads. Negative ads—spots that focus on criticism of one's opponent—may vary in important ways. Specifically, we propose that advertising may vary along a number of distinct dimensions, including how honest, how important, and how fair the charges made in ads seem to citizens. Such distinctions, we suggest, should play an important role in future studies of campaign advertising.

In arguing for this new perception-based approach to campaign advertising, we draw on three sets of data gathered during the 2000 U.S. Senate race in Virginia. These diverse data provide an unprecedented look at the campaign as it was experienced by citizens in the Commonwealth. We draw first on ad tracking data provided by the Campaign Media Analysis Group (CMAG), which we use to present a detailed picture of advertising in the Virginia race. We then introduce a new methodology for evaluating campaign advertising: on-line coding of actual campaign ads by real citizens, who viewed the ads over the Internet, in the privacy of their own homes. We use these evaluations to demonstrate the ways in which perceptions of campaign ads—even "negative" ads—can vary. Finally, we draw on a four-wave panel study of Virginia citizens to describe citizen attitudes about the candidates and their campaigns.

THE STUDY ON CAMPAIGN CONDUCT

In July of 2000, the Pew Charitable Trusts awarded a $730,000 grant to the Sorensen Institute for Political Leadership at the University of Virginia. The grant was intended to support the Institute's Project on Campaign Conduct, initiated in 1997 by an earlier grant from the Trusts. During the three-year grant period, the Sorensen Institute has been charged with the research and development of the Candidate Training Program, a training curriculum for state and local candidates who are seeking office for the first time.[2] To support its curriculum development, the Sorensen Institute has embarked upon a program of research to gain a clear understanding of how voters view campaigns and candidate behavior, along with the impact of campaign conduct on citizen attitudes and participation.

The 2000 U.S. Senate race in Virginia between Chuck Robb and George Allen provides the context for this study. The campaign was a hard-fought battle in which the stakes were high, the candidates were well known and well funded, and the competition was intense. As a result, the full range of campaign discourse was on display, from pointed but courteous "high-road" exchanges to good old, hard-hitting body blows.

THE DATA

CMAG AD TRACKING DATA

The first source of data for this study consists of detailed reports about each advertisement aired during the campaign. The reports, generated by the Campaign Media Analysis Group (CMAG), provide a daily accounting of the exact time each ad aired, during which TV program, on which television station, and in which media market. The system monitors advertising in the country's top 75 media markets, including the top four markets in Virginia.[3]

INTERNET AD TESTS

The second source of data consists of citizen perceptions of each ad that aired in the course of the 2000 campaign. Using a new technology developed by Market Strategies, a political market research firm, all fifty-three television commercials aired during the campaign were seen and evaluated by groups of at least fifty people over the Internet. For these "e-tests" more than 1,000 Virginia residents were recruited from the subscription list of Juno, a large provider of free e-mail and Internet services. Participants were offered a small monetary incentive and assigned to one of eleven e-test groups. Using streaming video, each respondent was shown a mixture of ads favoring or opposing each candidate, for a total of five campaign ads.

Participants in the e-tests were asked a battery of demographic questions as well as queries about partisanship, ideology, campaign attentiveness, political knowledge, candidate favorability, and vote choice. While watching the ad, respondents were asked to move their mouse along a scale from 0 to 10 (appearing at the bottom of the screen) to rate how much they liked or disliked what they saw in the ad. Following each ad, respondents were asked to rate the ad according to a negative-positive scale in addition to rating each ad for its fairness, importance, and honesty along a 0–10 point scale.

Not surprisingly, the universe of Juno users is not representative of all Virginians (although it is perhaps less skewed than one might expect).[4] Notwithstanding these slight biases, the e-tests represent an improvement over evaluations by traditional dial-test focus groups or coding by researchers or elite coders. Focus groups are generally much smaller, much more expensive, and restricted to participants recruited from the immediate vicinity of the focus group facility. In contrast, e-tests allow the researcher to show the campaign ads to a much larger, more diverse sample of people. Moreover, since respondents watch the ads and record their responses in the privacy of their own homes, their opinions are not influenced by the other participants in their e-test group or by the focus group leader.

PANEL STUDY OF VIRGINIANS

The final source of data is a four-wave panel study of voting-age citizens in Virginia. Respondents were interviewed three times before the election and once after. Interviewing took place in late August–early September, late September–early October, late October–early November, and then following the election. The postelection wave was supplemented with a fresh cross-section to help compensate for panel attrition and control for panel contamination.

The survey research focused on citizen perceptions of the race, in addition to questions about political participation, mobilization, campaign interest and attention, general political knowledge, trust and efficacy, candidate likes and dislikes, issue positions of respondents and perceived positions of candidates' partisanship, ideology, and vote choice. In addition, respondents were asked extensive batteries of questions about media use and television viewing habits to aid in estimating exposure to campaign advertisements.

The fourth wave of the panel study is of particular importance, as it includes postelection responses to questions about voter turnout and vote choice. The fourth wave was in the field from November 15 to December 7, 2000, and includes 465 respondents from the panel and a fresh cross-section of 408 new respondents, for a total n of 873.[5]

PRIOR RESEARCH ON CAMPAIGN ADVERTISING

Despite myriad studies on political advertising and its effects on voters, a considerable degree of uncertainty and disagreement remains. In particular, controversy surrounds a set of claims that negative advertising leads to diminished political efficacy and a demobilized electorate. Contradictory findings—stemming in part from an impressive range of methodological approaches—led Lau et al. to conclude in a recent meta-analysis "that prevailing understandings of the effects of negative political ads are in need of fundamental rethinking" (1999, 860). Certainly, among the factors contributing to the confusion is the problem of construct definition: Although we might know it when we see it, it is not clear just what a "negative ad" is, nor how best to classify political advertising.

Much of the research on the impact of campaign ads has been based on a simple, dichotomous approach to coding advertising: If the ad criticizes the opponent, it is coded as "negative." If the ad only contains information about the sponsor, it is coded as "positive." Such an approach is easy to employ and simple to replicate, but there are a number of disadvantages. For example, classifying an ad as simply negative or positive says very little about the ad's substantive content, or about how that content was perceived by potential voters. In addition, the breadth of these categories ensures that very diverse kinds of ads will be included in the same category. Ads that discuss an opponent's position on abortion or gun control will be coded as "negative," together with ads that assault the opponent's character or dredge up past personal indiscretions. Common sense alone suggests that voters may differ in their perceptions of campaign charges—possibly with considerable variation in how different kinds of "negative" ads affect voting behavior.

Although some researchers have developed variations on the dichotomous coding system (including multiple-category measures of tone and assorted attempts to distinguish between trait- and issue-focused ads), these alternatives share a common weakness: Each applies coding that the researchers themselves have designed and that therefore may be subject to their own preconceptions and biases. By contrast, we suggest that voters themselves are a better source of information about their perceptions of ads.

Relying on citizens to provide information about how they perceive campaign ads helps reduce the inherent subjectivity of elite coding, and provides a more valid measure of advertising tone in the eyes of the people who matter most: potential voters.

Such an approach is not completely new. In a 1989 article, Johnson-Cartee and Copeland proposed a perception-based measure of charges that are frequently used in campaign ads. They tested ten charges and found that voters do make distinctions between the fairness of different charges. Respondents saw charges about a candidate's issues positions and political record, for example, as being considerably more fair than charges about a candidate's family or sex life. In the present study, we build on the work of Johnson-Cartee and Copeland by focusing on citizens' *perceptions* of campaign advertising.[6]

ADVERTISING IN THE 2000 ELECTION

Outside of Virginia, the election of 2000 saw record levels of political advertising. Nationally, close to one million individual ads were broadcast by candidates, parties, and interest groups. In the presidential race alone, 245,165 general election spots were aired, a 48 percent increase over 1996 (Goldstein and Freedman 2002). This advertising was not, of course, evenly distributed throughout the nation. As one would expect, presidential ads were heavily targeted toward markets in the hard-fought battleground states. Viewers in the St. Louis market, for example, saw more than 7,900 general election ads for Bush or Gore, while residents of Detroit, Seattle, and Philadelphia were treated to more than 8,900 spots. Worst off in 2000 were the beleaguered Albuquerqueans, who were subjected to a barrage of more than 9,700 presidential ads.

In stark contrast, viewers in three of Virginia's top four media markets saw *not a single general election ad* for either Bush or Gore, while viewers in the Washington, D.C., market saw fewer than 300 spots throughout the election.[7] While there were a handful of general election spots broadcast outside the D.C. market for Buchanan (ten) and Libertarian candidate Harry Browne (four), advertising by the major political parties and their presidential candidates was literally nonexistent.

This is not to say, however, that Virginians were deprived of political advertising in 2000. To the contrary, the Richmond, Roanoke, Norfolk, and Washington, D.C., media markets were home to 39,870 political spots broadcast between January 1 and Election Day.[8] A third of these ads were aired during the Republican primary (5,299) and in House races (8,199). The vast majority, however, were broadcast during the Robb-Allen Senate race. All told, the candidates, parties, and outside interest groups produced fifty-four separate ads during the campaign, and as Table 6.1 on page 110 indicates, these spots were broadcast a total of 25,829 times in the top four media markets.

TABLE 6.1   VIRGINIA SENATE ADS AIRED BY SPONSOR

	ALLEN	ROBB	TOTAL
Candidates	7,010	5,083	12,093
Parties	5,301	6,731	12,032
Groups	300	1,404	1,704
Total	12,611	13,218	25,829

Source: Based on data from the Wisconsin Advertising Project.

About half of all the Senate ads aired in Virginia were produced by the candidates' own campaigns. Allen had a distinct advantage, broadcasting 7,010 spots during the course of the campaign, compared to 5,083 for Robb. However, with assistance from the Virginia Democratic Party (VADP) and sympathetic interest groups like the Sierra Club and the League of Conservation Voters, Robb was able to take the lead in total advertising. The VADP broadcast 6,731 spots on behalf of the incumbent senator, while the state GOP aired only 5,301 for Allen. Democratic-friendly interest groups broadcast 1,404 spots for Robb, compared to a mere 300 aired for Allen by the Chamber of Commerce, the NRA, and the National Pro-Life Alliance. All told, Robb led Allen in total advertising 13,218 spots to 12,611.

These spots were slightly more concentrated in the Commonwealth's two largest media markets. Just under 30 percent of all Senate ads were aired in the battleground of Northern Virginia (the Washington, D.C., media market), where Allen was determined to make inroads into Robb's core base of support. Another 27 percent were aired in the Norfolk market, 24 percent in Richmond, and 19 percent in Roanoke. These patterns differ somewhat from the distribution of total political advertising in the state: Because the lion's share of non-Senate advertising came from House races in the Norfolk and Richmond markets, a third of all political advertising in 2000 was in the Norfolk market, 28 percent in Richmond, 21 percent in Washington, and only 18 percent in Roanoke.

Allen was on the air early and often, taking a strong lead in the number of spots aired by the beginning of the summer (see Figure 6.1). Between the end of April and mid-June, Allen broadcast 240 spots, compared to only 10 for Robb (a Sierra Club spot). By the end of August, Allen had aired more than 1,500 ads, compared with fewer than 700 for Robb. This pattern changed dramatically in the fall, however. Starting in the end of September, Robb and his allies out-broadcast Allen every single week, by an average of 300 ads. During the last week of the campaign there was a particularly strong push by Robb, who took a 700-spot lead over Allen (2,672 to 1,950).

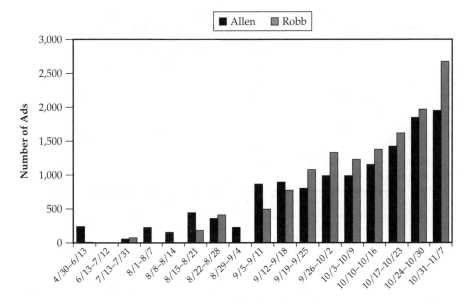

FIGURE 6.1   ADS AIRED BY WEEK

THE VIEW FROM THE GROUND 1:
CITIZEN PERCEPTIONS OF THE AD CAMPAIGN

What was the nature of the nearly 26,000 ads that confronted Virginians in the fall of 2000? Turning first to the most familiar measure of tone, we coded the Robb-Allen ads as either *attack, contrast,* or *promote.* Coders at the University of Wisconsin and University of Virginia examined storyboards and/or videotape for each of the fifty-three ads produced during the Senate campaign, and determined whether each spot contained only positive information about the sponsor (a promotional spot), only negative information about the opponent (an attack spot), or some combination (a contrast spot).[9]

Consistent with past findings (Freedman and Goldstein 1999), the majority (56.4 percent) of the Robb-Allen ads broadcast contained a mix of negative and positive information. An additional 26.2 percent were pure attack spots, and only 17.3 percent were solely promotional (see Table 6.2 on page 112). The patterns for the two candidates, however, were vastly different. As Table 6.2 illustrates, more than 35 percent of Robb's ads were pure attacks, more than double Allen's share (17 percent). The Allen camp was far more likely to air contrast spots than were Robb and his allies (63.5 percent of Allen's ads, vs. 49.6 percent of Robb's), and slightly more likely to run positive, self-promotional spots (a fifth of Allen's ads, vs. 15 percent of Robb's).[10]

TABLE 6.2   VIRGINIA SENATE ADS BY OBJECTIVE TONE

SPONSOR	ATTACK	CONTRAST	PROMOTE
Robb ads (total)	35.3	49.6	15.1
Allen ads (total)	16.8	63.5	19.7
Robb campaign	0.0	60.9	39.1
Allen campaign	9.1	55.5	35.4
VADP	58.8	41.2	0.0
VAGOP	24.1	76.0	0.0
Robb group	50.9	49.1	0.0
Allen group	69.7	30.3	0.0

Note: Cell entries are percentages; rows sum to 100%.

Source: Based on data from the Wisconsin Advertising Project.

To be sure, many of the contrast spots included hard-hitting attacks. Here, for example, is the script of one Allen ad that the campaign ran over 1,000 times in the top four media markets:

The Robb record: Doubled the parole rate in Virginia. Released violent offenders after they served as little as one-third of their prison time. Opposed tougher penalties for selling cocaine. Refused to let schools expel students who bring guns to the classroom.

George Allen abolished parole, increased penalties for criminals using guns, and brought crime to its lowest level in ten years. Now he wants an all-out war on drugs to take pushers off the streets and protect our kids. Leadership and Virginia values. George Allen for Senate.

Clearly, this contrast spot contains information that, on its own, would be classified as an unequivocal attack. And the Robb campaign was tough in its contrast ads as well, as illustrated by this ad about the environment, which ran nearly 800 times in the state's top markets:

As governor, Chuck Robb signed a landmark Chesapeake Bay Agreement. In the Senate, he supported the Clean Air & Water Act and fought to protect Virginia from out of state trash.

George Allen has a different record. He sued to overturn the Clean Air Act, refused to enforce environmental laws. Stood by while a campaign contributor polluted the tributary of the Chesapeake. And a nonpartisan group rated Allen's environmental record one of the worst in the nation. Senator Robb. An environmental record we can rely on.

Given our past research, we suspect that all contrast ads—like all attack ads—are not created equal. The amount of time devoted to each candidate, the intensity of the charges, the visual imagery, even the music employed can produce substantial differences in how spots are actually perceived by viewers. Indeed, we suspect that there may be greater differences in perceived tone *within* the categories of attack and contrast than *between* them.

To what extent do such differences in perceptions actually exist? In order to better gauge citizens' responses to political advertising, we turn to the results of our on-line ad tests. (A complete list of each ad made, along with ratings, appears as Appendix A. The full text of selected ads appears as Appendix B.) First, we consider our measure of perceived tone. E-test participants were asked to evaluate the tone of each Robb-Allen spot, taken as a whole. On average, Robb's ads were seen as more negative than Allen's: The mean perception of Robb's ads was 4.4 (on a ten-point scale) while the mean for Allen's ads was 5.0 (Table 6.3). These overall scores, however, mask considerable variation based on ad sponsor: Spots aired by the campaigns themselves were considered to be the most positive (5.3 for Robb, 5.8 for Allen), while party ads were slightly more negative (4.0 for the VADP and 4.1 for the VAGOP), and interest group ads were seen as most negative of all (Robb's allies had a mean rating of 3.3, vs. 2.6 for Allen-friendly groups).

Similar patterns emerge for ratings of fairness, relevance, and perceived honesty (see Table 6.3 below and Figure 6.2 on page 114). Citizens perceived Robb's ads as being less fair on average than Allen's (with mean scores of 4.9 and 5.2), although the two candidates were more evenly matched when it came to perceptions of importance (6.9 for both) and honesty (5.1 for Robb, 5.2 for Allen). Once again, the candidates' own advertising received consistently higher ratings (i.e., more fair, more important, more honest) than party and interest group spots. In part, this pattern allows candidates themselves

TABLE 6.3   ON-LINE EVALUATIONS OF VIRGINIA SENATE ADS

	TONE	FAIRNESS	IMPORTANCE	HONESTY
Robb ads	4.4	4.9	6.9	5.1
Allen ads	5.0	5.2	6.9	5.2
Robb campaign	5.3	5.5	7.0	5.4
Allen campaign	5.8	5.9	7.1	5.6
VADP	4.0	4.4	6.9	4.9
VAGOP	4.1	4.3	6.7	4.8
Robb group	3.3	1.3	6.6	4.7
Allen group	2.6	3.9	6.9	4.5

Note: Cell entries are mean ratings, on a 0–10 scale.

Source: Based on data from the Wisconsin Advertising Project and Internet Dial Tests.

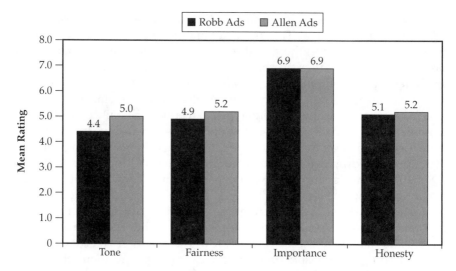

FIGURE 6.2 MEAN RATINGS OF ROBB AND ALLEN ADS BROADCAST

to take the relative "high road." To the extent that parties and interest groups shouldered a portion of each candidate's dirty work, Robb and Allen were able to dedicate more of their own time and money promoting themselves in positive terms.

Finally, perceptions of fairness, honesty, and relevance are correlated with perceptions of tone, as well as with the more objective positive-contrast-promote coding. Of the Robb-Allen ads produced in 2000, all of the attack spots were seen as less fair than the promotional ads, and all of the promotional spots were coded "fair." However, as we anticipated, there was a good deal of variation when it came to the contrast spots. Although a majority of the contrast spots produced were seen as "moderately fair" by our coders and more than a quarter were considered "fair," a full 22 percent were seen as "unfair."

A Focus on Education

The Robb-Allen Senate race featured advertising that touched on a range of topics, including gun control, crime, abortion, and the environment. The most prominent issue appearing in ads during the campaign, however, was education. Eight of the top ten most frequently aired ads mentioned the issue, and three of the top ten spots dealt with it exclusively. All told, there were eight spots (broadcast more than 7,300 times) that were devoted completely to the issue of education, and a total of twenty-one ads (broadcast more than 13,300 times during the campaign) that mentioned the issue in some way.

Among the eight ads focusing exclusively on education, Robb had the distinct advantage. Six of the eight were sponsored by the Robb campaign or the VADP, and were broadcast a total of 4,500 times. In contrast, only three of the education spots were sponsored by Allen or the VAGOP, and these were broadcast only 2,800 times. Robb's advantage in volume of education ads, however was offset by the higher ratings garnered by the Allen education ads. To an even greater extent than in the 2000 Senate advertising in general, the education spots aired by Allen and the Republicans were seen as more positive, more fair, more honest, and more important than the education ads broadcast by Robb and the Democrats (Figure 6.3). One of Allen's education spots, in fact, was seen as the most fair of all the ads aired during the race.

THE VIEW FROM THE GROUND 2: CITIZEN PERCEPTIONS OF THE CAMPAIGN

What did citizens think about the campaign in general? The panel study provides a detailed look at citizens' perceptions of the race at four times during the campaign. As described previously, after the initial interview in late August–early September, we reinterviewed respondents in late September–early October, late October–early November, and then again after the election in November. This allowed us to observe changes in citizens' attitudes about the race over the course of the campaign, as the ad war unfolded.

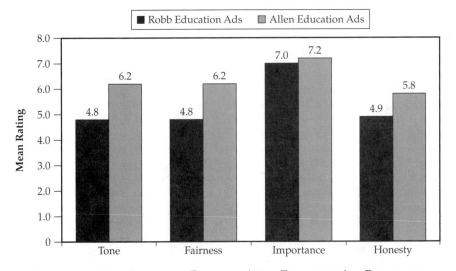

FIGURE 6.3   MEAN RATINGS OF ROBB AND ALLEN EDUCATION ADS BROADCAST

Survey respondents were asked a series of questions designed to probe their opinions about the race in general as well as each of the two campaigns. In addition, we inquired about how much attention they were paying to the race and whether they could recall seeing any campaign ads on television. The results appear in the following figures.

Figure 6.4 shows a steady increase in attention to both the presidential campaign and the Senate campaign. Not surprisingly, more people were paying attention to the presidential than to the Senate campaign throughout the election season. In August, for example, a slim majority of Virginians—55 percent—reported paying close attention to the presidential election. Less than half that, however—only 25 percent—were paying attention to the Senate race. This percentage grew steadily as the race unfolded, however. By November, more than 50 percent of respondents indicated that they were paying a "great deal" or "quite a bit" of attention to the Senate race, and more than three-quarters were watching the presidential race closely.

Figure 6.5 shows how respondents' perceptions of the Senate race changed over time. In each wave of the survey, we asked respondents to describe the race in terms of three sets of adjectives: negative or positive, exciting or boring, and informative or uninformative. As might be expected given the how little attention people paid to the Senate race in August, a relatively small percentage of respondents (9 percent) described the race as "exciting" and just over a quarter (26 percent) said they saw it as "informative." Even so, even at this early date, nearly a third (32 percent) described the race as being "negative."

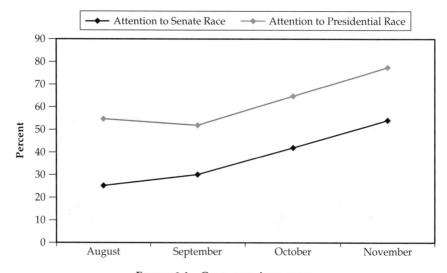

FIGURE 6.4   CAMPAIGN ATTENTION

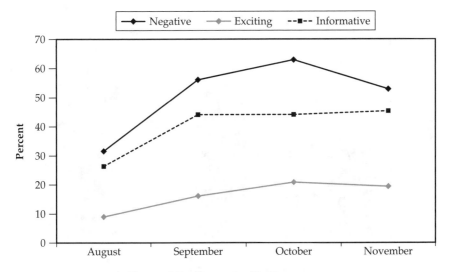

FIGURE 6.5 CAMPAIGN DESCRIPTIONS

By late September–early October, respondents found the race slightly more exciting (16 percent) and considerably more informative (44 percent). But the largest increase was in those respondents who described the race as being negative; this group grew by nearly 25 percentage points, to 56 percent. During the remainder of the campaign there was little change in the percentage of respondents who described the race as being informative and exciting. After the Labor Day boost, reflected in the September wave, the campaign did little to generate enthusiasm among voters. Still, perceptions of negativity continued to grow through the late October interview, peaking at 63 percent in the hard-hitting weeks immediately before the election. While there was a drop in assessments of negativity in the postelection wave, we suspect that this may have more to do with the race being over than with an actual change in the advertising climate at the end of the race.

The increase in perceived negativity during the course of the Senate race mirrors patterns of campaign ad recall. As shown in Figure 6.6 on page 118, the percentage of respondents who report having seen a campaign ad for Allen or Robb grows steadily over the course of the campaign, from under 50 percent in August, to more than 87 percent by late October. (The ad recall question was not asked in the postelection wave.)

Respondents who said they could recall an ad were asked to characterize as negative or positive the ad they remembered most clearly. Once again, perceptions of negativity increased with the approach of Election Day. In August only 48 percent of those who recalled having seen an ad described it as negative. By late October, 61 percent of those who reported having seen a campaign ad described the ad as negative.

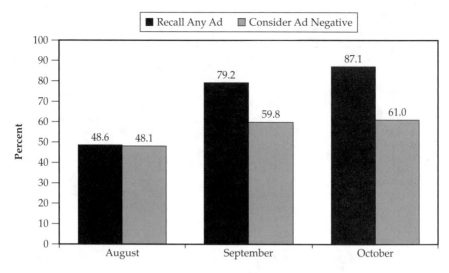

FIGURE 6.6   AD RECALL

The next two figures illustrate public perceptions of the Robb and Allen campaigns individually along four dimensions: fairness, honesty, tone (positive or negative), and effectiveness (Figures 6.7 and 6.8). Overall, these assessments confirm the findings from the on-line ad testing presented earlier. The Allen campaign was perceived as being generally more fair

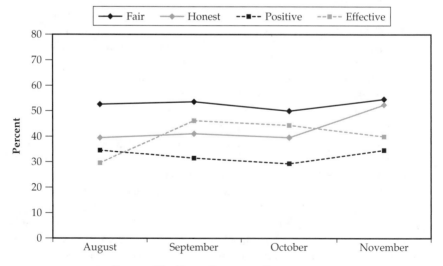

FIGURE 6.7   ROBB CAMPAIGN PERCEPTIONS

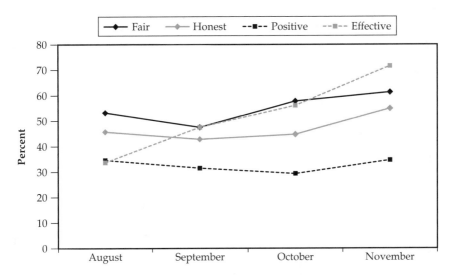

FIGURE 6.8   ALLEN CAMPAIGN PERCEPTIONS

and more honest than the Robb campaign, in addition to being perceived as being about equally positive. Particularly striking is the evidence that Allen's campaign was perceived as being more effective than Robb's from the beginning (34 percent described Allen's campaign as effective in August; 30 percent described Robb's campaign that way), a contrast that grew as the race progressed. By October, Robb's perceived effectiveness had peaked (at 46 percent in September) and began to slide (44 percent in October.) Meanwhile, Allen's perceived effectiveness took off: 48 percent described his race as effective in September and 56 percent did so in October, and a full 72 percent considered his campaign effective by the end of the race (not surprising, as respondents were presumably aware of the election outcome).

Allen's greater perceived effectiveness is mirrored in his consistently higher favorability ratings (Figure 6.9 on page 120). Allen had already established an early lead by August, with 62 percent saying that they had a "very favorable" or "somewhat favorable" opinion of him, while only 54 percent said the same of Robb. And Allen's favorability ratings increased slightly but steadily over the course of the campaign (as did public perceptions of him as being "hardworking" and "moral"). By contrast, the Robb campaign failed to energize the public: Robb's favorability ratings stagnated and then dropped slightly in the final weeks of the campaign. (Moreover, while citizens saw him as more hardworking in November than they had in August, perceptions of Robb's other attributes remained steady or dropped by the end of the campaign.)

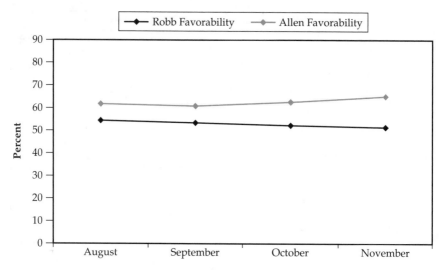

FIGURE 6.9 CANDIDATE FAVORABILITY

CONCLUSION

Our findings offer important lessons for how we study campaign advertising. For many purposes it is both necessary and appropriate to assign campaign ads to a small number of clearly defined coding categories, based on relatively objective criteria. For other purposes, however, such an approach is insufficient and may even lead to misleading inferences. When it comes to the effects of campaign ads on citizens' attitudes and behaviors, it may be more relevant to take into account how citizens themselves perceive such advertising.

This is precisely what we have attempted to do in this chapter. By combining the WiscAds information with the on-line ad tests and the survey data, we have assembled a comprehensive dataset that allows us to examine real ads, coded by real citizens, in the context of a real campaign. Citizens, we find, make careful and sometimes subtle distinctions in their evaluations of campaign advertising, distinctions that go beyond positive versus negative. When viewing television ads, citizens can and do discriminate on the basis of how important, honest, relevant, and fair the spots seem to them. These distinctions should help guide political scientists and others in future studies of campaign advertising.

Sponsor	Creative/Title	Mean Important	Mean Fair	Mean Honest	Mean Positive	Start Day	Count
Allen	Influential Governor	7.01	6.47	5.75	6.29	5/31	770
Allen	Isn't It Absurd	7.62	**7.33**	6.38	7.18	9/7	1278
Allen	Big Difference	6.67	4.95	5.29	5.04	9/20	719
Allen	Robb Out of Touch	7.02	4.48	4.55	5.19	10/2	668
Allen	Distorting Record on Education	7.45	6.63	6.09	7.01	10/6	704
Allen	Crime Drugs	7.20	5.28	5.31	4.86	10/11	1061
Allen	Abortion	6.59	5.61	5.55	4.99	10/19	294
Allen	Promise of SS	6.85	3.88	4.76	2.47	10/20	640
Allen	John Warner Endorsement	6.41	6.61	5.77	6.93	10/26	114
Allen	John Warner Endorsement 2	6.72	7.15	6.32	7.20	10/27	141
Allen	Sue Allen	6.80	6.04	6.19	7.19	11/1	112
Allen	I Trust You	7.61	6.42	6.02	7.39	11/2	444
Allen	Bush Endorsement	6.84	6.56	6.11	**8.05**	11/2	65
VAGOP	Robb Speak	6.37	3.63	4.60	3.75	8/15	1108
VAGOP	More Robb Speak	5.97	3.53	4.42	3.74	8/30	307
VAGOP	Even More Robb Speak	6.71	4.36	4.76	4.76	9/8	357
VAGOP	Robb Tell the Truth	6.49	4.56	4.91	4.44	9/14	826
VAGOP	Issue Welfare	6.44	4.59	5.15	4.78	9/27	569
VAGOP	Allen Facts on Gun Violence	7.71	5.19	5.06	4.90	10/6	933
VAGOP	Clinton-Robb Tax Agenda	6.38	4.18	4.57	3.16	10/18	553
VAGOP	Robb Traffic Record	6.36	4.36	4.98	3.60	10/25	233
VAGOP	Robb The Issue Is Trust	7.19	3.73	4.17	2.65	10/27	254
VAGOP	Robb Military Cuts	6.88	3.98	4.61	2.47	10/27	161
Robb	Good Man	*5.59*	5.91	5.61	6.25	9/15	245
Robb	Across Party Lines	7.39	6.40	5.65	6.22	9/20	1209
Robb	Education Governor	7.62	5.30	5.37	5.12	10/4	608
Robb	Education Plan	7.26	4.61	4.56	4.27	10/11	786
Robb	Allen Shoot Straight	6.72	4.93	5.14	4.42	10/18	545
Robb	Chesapeake Bay	6.08	4.57	4.86	4.28	10/23	793
Robb	Help Law Enforcement	7.35	5.95	5.62	5.11	10/25	130
Robb	Right to Choose	7.69	4.83	5.42	3.60	11/1	234
Robb	Tough Fight	7.32	7.32	**6.90**	7.53	11/2	533
VADP	Allen Isn't It Sad	6.58	5.71	5.61	5.63	8/18	643
VADP	Allen Education Record	6.63	4.08	4.56	4.16	9/4	676
VADP	Allen GMU President	6.04	4.05	4.38	3.90	9/13	562
VADP	Allen I Know the Facts	6.80	4.24	5.03	5.09	9/19	663
VADP	Who Is Real George Allen	5.99	3.47	4.23	3.67	9/26	1050
VADP	Facts GA Guns	7.71	5.01	5.39	4.82	10/5	683
VADP	Can VA Trust Allen on Healthcare	6.75	4.18	4.38	3.34	10/6	437
VADP	Allen Budget Doesn't Add Up	6.89	4.10	4.20	3.00	10/17	229
VADP	Allen NVA Roads	6.35	4.48	4.65	3.22	10/18	198
VADP	Allen Facts on Choice	7.63	5.19	5.67	4.02	10/24	523
VADP	Allen Issue: A Woman's Choice	7.76	5.39	5.58	3.94	10/27	506
VADP	Allen Outside VA Mainstream	7.60	3.85	4.74	*1.66*	11/1	561
COC	Robb Big Govt Rx Plan	6.89	*3.45*	4.28	1.94	10/27	194
NPLA	Robb Abortion 60	**8.40**	5.05	5.51	3.09	10/12	15
NRA	Other Countries Allen	6.44	4.41	4.53	3.80	10/24	42
NRA	Heston Gig Is up Allen	6.73	4.91	4.81	4.18	10/24	49
Sierra	Allen Cut Funds	7.13	4.64	5.15	4.30	4/30	10
Sierra	Robb Clean Water	7.47	5.06	5.24	3.97	11/1	110
LCV	Allen Dump	6.74	3.51	*4.16*	2.14	10/18	436
LCV	Allen Toxic River	7.16	3.95	4.51	1.95	10/18	230
VFC	Check the Record	6.15	5.03	5.11	4.69	10/19	543

Note: Highest score in each category denoted in bold; lowest score in bold italic.

Sponsors: Allen: Allen Campaign, VAGOP: Virginia Republican Party, Robb: Robb Campaign, VADP: Virginia Democratic Party, COC: Chamber of Commerce, NPLA: National Pro-Life Association, NRA: National Rifle Association, Sierra: Sierra Club, LCV: League of Conservation Voters, VFC: Voters for Choice.

APPENDIX B: SELECTED 2000 VIRGINIA SENATE CAMPAIGN AD SCRIPTS

Sponsor: Allen
Title: *Isn't It Absurd*
Start Date: 9/7
Number of Times Ran: 1,278
Ratings:
  Important: 7.62
  Fair: 7.33 (most fair)
  Honest: 6.38
  Positive: 7.18
Script: [Allen]: "Isn't it absurd what some people say, just to stay in Washington? Heck, our own children attend public schools. Just like you, Susan and I want them to get a quality education. As governor, I invested two billion new dollars to raise academic standards, improve reading, make our schools safe, and hire more teachers to reduce class sizes. As senator, I'll fight for a $1,000 education opportunity tax credit for every child in Virginia and America."

Sponsor: Allen
Title: *Bush Endorsement*
Start Date: 11/2
Number of Times Ran: 65
Ratings:
  Important: 6.84
  Fair: 6.56
  Honest: 6.11
  Positive: 8.05 (most positive)
Script: [Bush]: "Hello, I'm Governor George W. Bush. George Allen is my friend. He's a decent, honest man who'll work hard for common sense conservative values in the U.S. Senate. Like an early reading initiative so that no child is left behind. Rebuilding our military with better pay and morale for those who protect our freedom. Tax cuts for all taxpayers. George Allen kept his word as your governor: Now, America needs his leadership in the Senate. I would appreciate your vote for George Allen."

Sponsor: Robb
Title: *Good Man*
Start Date: 9/15
Number of Times Ran: 245
Ratings:
  Important: 5.59 (least important)
  Fair: 5.91

Honest: 5.61

Positive: 6.25

Script: [Announcer]: The courage to do what's right when it's not popular. Why do some men volunteer to risk their lives for their beliefs? Is it born out of idealism? Or does it arise from the ability to see what's right before others see it? To forecast the judgment of history? To see justice where some see hate and hope where others see fear? Or is it simply steadiness during the time of conflict and confusion? Whatever it is, it's what sets some men apart and what makes a good man a respected senator.

Sponsor: Robb

Title: *Tough Fight*

Start Date: 11/2

Number of Times Ran: 533

Ratings:

Important: 7.32

Fair: 7.32

Honest: 6.90 (most honest)

Positive: 7.53

Script: [Robb]: "Being in a tough fight builds character. I learned that when I fought in Vietnam and in some tough political battles here in Virginia. I want to keep on fighting for a stronger America, militarily and economically. And I want everyone included. That's why I fought so hard for better schools, a cleaner environment, and common sense gun safety laws. That's why I am so committed to civil rights, human rights, and a woman's right to choose. You may not agree with me on every issue but you know I work hard and I'll vote my convictions. Some important principles are on the line. Please don't forget to vote."

Sponsor: VADP

Title: *Allen Outside VA Mainstream*

Start Date: 11/1

Number of Times Ran: 561

Ratings:

Important: 7.60

Fair: 3.85

Honest: 4.74

Positive: 1.66 (least positive)

Script: [Announcer]: George Allen. A record outside Virginia's mainstream. The only governor to refuse Goals2000 education funding. Voted three times against family leave, giving mothers time off to care for their new babies. Cut prescription drug benefits for the poor seniors. Against a woman's right to choose and 1 of 6 legislators to vote against the minimum wage. Check the facts about the real George Allen.

Sponsor: COC
Title: *Robb Big Govt Rx Plan*
Start Date: 10/27
Number of Times Ran: 194
Ratings:
  Important: 6.89
  Fair: 3.45 (least fair)
  Honest: 4.28
  Positive: 1.94
Script: [Announcer]: Senator Robb supports a big-government prescription drug plan that could be costly for seniors. This plan requires seniors to pay up to $600 plus a 50/50 copayment. In this big-government plan, seniors have a one-time chance to sign up, otherwise they face penalties to join later. And who would decide which medicines are covered and which aren't? Tell Senator Robb to stop scaring seniors. Tell him to stop supporting a big-government prescription drug plan.

Sponsor: NPLA
Title: *Robb Abortion 60*
Start Date: 10/12
Number of Times Ran: 15
Ratings:
  Important: 8.40 (most important)
  Fair: 5.05
  Honest: 5.51
  Positive: 3.09
Script: [Announcer]: America was outraged when two New Jersey teenagers checked into a Delaware hotel and delivered and disposed of their newborn baby in a dumpster. Most Americans couldn't believe that defenseless human life could be so coldly snuffed out. But incredibly, if a doctor had been present that day in Delaware, and delivered the infant, all but one inch from full birth, and then killed him it would have been perfectly legal. Instead of murder or manslaughter, it would have been called a partial birth abortion. Killing late in the third trimester, killing just inches from full birth, partial birth abortion inflicts a violent death on thousands of babies every year. Your senator, Chuck Robb, voted to continue this grisly procedure. Contact Senator Robb

today and insist that he change his vote and oppose partial birth abortion. His number in Washington is (202) 224–3121. Again, his number is (202) 224–3121. Paid for by members of the National Pro-Life Alliance.

Sponsor: LCV
Title: *Allen Dump*
Start Date: 10/18
Number of Times Ran: 436
Ratings:
   Important: 6.74
   Fair: 3.51
   Honest: 4.16 (least honest)
   Positive: 2.14
Script: [Announcer]: It's one of the worst toxic waste dumps in the nation, right on a Virginia college campus. But as governor, George Allen blocked its cleanup, siding with developers instead. The Army Corp of Engineers called it catastrophic. But it was nothing new for Allen, the same governor who allowed more toxic dumping than thirty-four other states, a record the press termed shameful and out of step. That is why Allen has been named to the dirty dozen. His record is one of the worst. George Allen puts polluters first.

REFERENCES

Ansolabehere, Stephen, Shanto Iyengar, Adam Simon, and Nicholas Valentino. "Does Attack Advertising Demobilize the Electorate?" *American Political Science Review* 88 (1994): 829–838.

Ansolabehere, Stephen, and Shanto Iyengar. *Going Negative: How Political Advertisements Shrink and Polarize the Electorate.* New York: Free Press, 1995.

Ansolabehere, Stephen, Shanto Iyengar, and Adam Simon. "Replicating Experiments Using Aggregate and Survey Data: The Case of Negative Advertising and Turnout." *American Political Science Review* 93 (1999): 901–909.

Finkel, Steven E., and John G. Geer. "A Spot Check: Casting Doubt on the Demobilizing Effect of Attack Advertising." *American Journal of Political Science* 42 (1998): 573–595.

Freedman, Paul, Dale Lawton, and William Wood. "Do's and Don'ts of Negative Advertising: What Voters Say about Attack Politics," in *The Good Fight: How Political Candidates Struggle to Win Elections without Losing Their Souls.* Ed. Ronald A. Faucheux and Paul S. Herrnson. Washington, D.C.: Campaigns and Elections, 2001.

Freedman, Paul, and Ken Goldstein. "Measuring Media Exposure and the Effects of Negative Campaign Ads." *American Journal of Political Science* 43 (October 1999): 1189–1208.

Goldstein, Ken, and Paul Freedman. "Lessons Learned: Campaign Advertising in the 2000 Elections." *Political Communication* 19 (2002): 5–28.

Johnson-Cartee, Karen S., and Gary Copeland. "Southern Voters' Response to Negative Political Ads in 1986 Election." *Journalism Quarterly* 66 (1989): 888–986.

Lau, Richard R., Lee Sigelman, Caroline Heldman, and Paul Babbitt. "The Effects of Negative Political Advertisements: A Meta-Analytic Assessment." *American Political Science Review* 93 (1999): 851–875.

NOTES

1. This research was supported with a grant from the Pew Charitable Trusts. We would like to thank the following people for their help with this project: Bill Wood, Alison Meloy, T. J. Posey, Lindsay Forehand, Amy Spitler, Ken Goldstein, Greg Smith, Tom Guterbock, Brian Meekins, the staff of the Center for Survey Research, and the Chuck Robb and George Allen Senate campaigns.

2. The program, designed as a three-day workshop, provides a foundation of basic campaign-related skills while focusing on ethical campaign conduct and the effect of various campaign tactics on the public. Since receiving the first grant in 1997, the institute has sponsored three sessions of the Candidate Training Program, each involving approximately eighteen candidates for office in Virginia. Over the remaining two years of the current grant, the institute is working to refine the curriculum and begin collaborating with partners to sponsor the program in at least three other states.

3. Although there are over 200 media markets in the United States, over 80 percent of the population lives in the top seventy-five markets. In Virginia, approximately 90 percent of the population lives in one of the top four markets (Washington, D.C., Richmond, Norfolk, and Roanoke).

4. Compared with data from the U.S. Census, Virginia's Juno users are more likely to be male (57 percent) than Virginians at large (49 percent), wealthier (only a third make less than $30,000 a year, compared to 42 percent of the population in general), and a little older (40 percent of Juno subscribers are under forty, versus 44 percent of Virginians.)

5. All of the surveys were conducted by the University of Virginia's Center for Survey Research. The surveys employed a list-assisted RDD sample for initial panel selection and for the fresh cross-section in wave IV. Panel participants were given a small monetary incentive. We used a last-birthday method to randomly select registered respondents within households. The panel and cross-section data have been weighted to reflect the demographic composition of the Commonwealth.

6. In past work we employed an experimental research design to explore more precisely the relationship between campaign criticism and turnout (Freedman, Lawton, and Wood 2001). Drawing on two telephone surveys of citizens in Virginia conducted in 1998 and 1999, we investigated perceptions of campaign criticism, and asked whether such perceptions mattered for voter turnout. We found that in a series of experimental campaign vignettes, the impact of campaign messages on reported vote intention was dependent upon the nature and mix of messages the respondent was exposed to. Being exposed to an exchange of fair criticisms lead to a much higher probability of voting than exposure to an exchange of moderate criticisms. In contrast, exposure to an exchange of unfair attacks led to the lowest level of intended turnout. In general, we found that estimated turnout rose as the fairness of charges and countercharges increased: for any given charge, turnout tended to be higher when the countercharge was more fair, lower when the counter was less fair. We take these findings as establishing probable cause for the hypothesis that perceptions of fairness may matter for voter turnout in the context of an actual election campaign.

7. These ads, broadcast exclusively in the Washington, D.C., market, were aired by interest groups on behalf of Bush (14 spots) or Gore (251 spots).

8. This figure includes ads determined to have an election objective, and does not include approximately 2,600 genuine "issue advocacy" ads aired mainly in the Washington, D.C., market.

9. The UVa and Wisconsin coders agreed perfectly in forty-six out of fifty-three cases. Most of the disagreements involved contrast ads that had been improperly coded as attack spots by one coder. These disagreements were resolved by the authors; all were classified as contrast spots.

10. Note that the data in this table and those that follow reflect the spots actually aired, rather than simply the ads produced by the campaigns, parties, and groups.

PAY TO PLAY

PARTIES, INTERESTS, AND MONEY IN FEDERAL ELECTIONS

DAVID C. W. PARKER AND JOHN J. COLEMAN

Campaign finance is one of many areas on which the U.S. Constitution is silent. The Constitution provides for the election of federal officials, but says very little about how the process should work. Where would candidates be found? How would voters be informed? How would it all be funded? Political parties emerged partly to answer these questions, particularly the first two, and from the start private interests have been part of the answer to the third question. But what has been the electoral relationship between parties, candidates, and interests historically? Political scientists often posit an inverse relationship between political parties and interest groups—when parties, the representatives of broad, aggregate interests, are strong, narrowly-based interest groups are weak (Richardson 1995; Schattschneider 1960). To some extent, this story is satisfactory. In certain periods, for example, parties dominated the campaign landscape, grooming candidates, communicating with voters, and raising money—effectively diminishing the roles of individual candidates and private interests. In other periods, parties have acted as service organizations for candidates, with interest groups exercising considerable clout resulting from their organizational and financial strength.

There are, however, at least two problems with this account. First, there are periods in which parity might best define the relationship between parties and interests. Second, even for those periods in which an inverse relationship appears to hold, the standard account does little to explain *why* this relationship is inverse. To address these two shortcomings, we begin with the premise that parties, candidates, and interests desire power and influence. The purpose of that power and influence might be strictly personal—

reelection, for example—or it might be more systemic and social, such as advancing a particular vision of the proper ordering of social, economic, and political life. One way to obtain power and influence is through elections, and that is the focus of our attention. For candidates, victory can lead to personal influence. For parties, legislative majorities, or at least large minorities, greatly assist the exercise of influence. For interests, influencing those in elected office and influencing *who* is elected to office can further their agendas. Interests need the assistance of public officials and, on the flip side, political parties and candidates require resources to corral the necessary votes for victory. Those resources might well be dispensed by organized interests. We argue that the relationship between parties, interest groups, and individual candidates depends upon the electoral resources necessary for political victory at a given historical juncture and how dependent parties are on interest groups for those resources.

To understand the pulling and hauling between political parties, interests, and candidates, we examine the evolution of the electoral and monetary rules of the game. Are there any recurrent patterns in the parade of reforms that affect the parties-interests-candidates triad? We suggest there are at least four. First, and perhaps most obvious, reforms follow perceived corruption or scandals in the electoral process. Second, significant expansion or contraction of the national state is a critical catalyst for campaign finance abuses and reforms. Third, there has been an increasing willingness by private interests to use independent means to influence the electoral process. And fourth, the relative strength of parties, groups, and candidates in the electoral process depends on the need for resources and on the scale of mobilization deemed necessary for victory. We first present an overview of the reforms and then discuss each of these themes in more detail.

THE FIRST REFORMS: MUGWUMPS AND PROGRESSIVES

The connection between private money and public politics was not always a political issue around which major political movements formed. With the rise of the mass political party and political machines in the 1830s, charges of corruption might hound a party or politicians in particular cities and states. A national organized movement to reform the relationship between parties, interest groups, and money, however, would not emerge until the late nineteenth century. Why then? The key reason is that the expanded activity of government greatly increased the centrality of the state to the fortunes of private actors. With this increased centrality came more political activism by organized interests, and with this activism came new perceptions of corruption.

In this period of major transition, middle class citizens were uneasy with

> the new scale of the cities, the trusts, and the financial giants, rising around them like colossi from dragons' teeth. The shame [Muckrakers and Progressives generally] decried . . . was the purchase of public power for private ends, the degeneration of politics into a mere auction house for interested bidders. Before the eyes of the startled readers of the slick, new, middle-class magazines, the muckrakers unveiled the mechanisms of a commodified politics. The world they revealed was one in which . . . the State itself had been put up for sale, transformed into a thriving, open market for private interests. (Rodgers 1987: 180)

The word "interests" emerged in the Progressive Era to describe the penetration of money and private power into politics. "The Interests were, by definition, alien and predatory: sores on the body politic" (Rodgers 1987, 181–182). The reformers of the age, at first Mugwumps and later Progressives or Muckrakers, sought reestablishment of a politics of the center—a politics of the "best men," of those sober, enlightened individuals who were guided by the social welfare rather than selfish or narrow interests (Miller 1983: 85). The reformers' concerns resonated with Americans weaned on the republican, antifactional ideology of the early United States. Having grown from commerce and trade, interests were inherently suspect (Miller 1983, 11). With the franchise open to all males whether or not they owned real estate, and reins of government held increasingly by party professionals rather than an aristocratic elite, those who perceived themselves as beyond the petty concerns of commerce developed a fear of the corrupting potential of private monetary interests. Even those engaged in commerce, the alleged source of corrupting interests, feared money's corrosive influence. Although there was no single business interest—some preferred tariffs, others did not, manufacturers and railroads were frequently at odds, and so on (Miller 1983, 88)—there was always a fear that someone wealthier and savvier would arrange a better deal with government. In the end, the balancing act between interests, parties, and individual politicians was intricate and complicated. How money related to influence depended on how candidates and parties marshaled the resources necessary for political victory.

Even before a political movement emerged, however, there was federal reform of campaign financing. Reform first appeared after the Civil War, in the Naval Appropriations Bill of 1867. This bill banned the solicitation of naval yard workers by officers and employees of the government. More significantly, the conduct of local and state political machines during the 1870s and 1880s instigated the first major round of political finance reform. The corruption and graft of party machines such as New York's Tweed Ring and Philadelphia's Gas Ring are legendary. In New York City under Boss Tweed, "contractors expected to pay 10 percent of a contract to the political machine" (Griffith 1974, 70). Worse than kickbacks were the city ordinances designed to wrest money from businesses. City officials' enforcement of various regulations was—to be generous—flexible. Businessmen who may have committed no violation found their shops closed or heavy penalties levied if they did not contribute a kickback to the machine (Callow 1965, 191).[1]

The excesses of Boss Tweed and the perceived inefficiency of machine government spurred the creation of the New York Civil Service Reform Association in 1880 and demands for the establishment of a merit-based system in government bureaucracy. Controlled by business interests and the emerging professional middle class, the reform movement spread rapidly throughout the states and by 1881 merged into a national organization (Schiesl 1977). The Mugwumps (as the reformers were known) triumphed when President Chester Arthur signed the Pendleton Act into law in 1882. While improving the efficiency and professional nature of the civil service, the Pendleton Act also seriously undermined the financial resources of political parties. No longer could elected officials count on assessments (monetary kickbacks) of officeholders to fill their coffers, as the law forbade assessments by federal career civil service officials. Although candidate assessments still provided some of the monies necessary to conduct elections and mobilize voters, parties needed new revenue sources.

The most obvious place to turn was big business. The Pendleton Act's passage had the consequence of increasing the stature of business in the electoral process. "Business became a prime source of campaign funds [and] some large corporations gave regularly to both parties in order to buy protection and favors" (Thayer 1973, 38). The increasing need for money in an era of escalating campaign costs—resulting from the expansion of the franchise, the development of new communications technology, and the beginning of the advertising era in campaigns (McGerr 1986)—led party financiers essentially to levy businesses.[2] In the 1896 presidential election, McKinley campaign manager Mark Hanna took money raising to new heights. According to various estimates, the Republican National Committee raised some $3 to $3.5 million, the equivalent of about $60 to $70 million in the year 2000, on behalf of McKinley's campaign (Subcommittee of the Committee on Privileges and Elections 1912, hereafter referred to as the Clapp Committee Hearings 1912; Overacker 1932; Pollock 1926). Much of this money Hanna raised himself with the assistance of railroad tycoon (and Democrat) James Hill.[3]

The 1904 presidential election brought the issue of campaign finance into full public view. Late in the fall campaign, Democratic presidential aspirant Alton B. Parker charged Roosevelt campaign chairman, Georges

Cortelyou, of using his cabinet position to wrest campaign money for the Republican effort. Roosevelt vigorously denied the rumors at the time and eight years later during the Clapp Hearings investigating the financing of the presidential contests of 1904, 1908, and the pre-convention campaign of 1912 (Clapp Committee Hearings 1912: 186). Similarly, Cortelyou flatly rejected the suggestion that any contribution was made on a quid pro quo basis (Clapp Committee Hearings 1912: 21).

Shortly after Parker leveled his charges, Roosevelt announced his support for eliminating corporate contributions to candidates for federal office in both his 1905 and 1906 State of the Union addresses. In 1907, after repeated attempts, Congress passed the Tillman Act to do just that. Corporate contributions to campaigns were outlawed and punishable by fine and imprisonment.

The fervor over corporate donations in the 1904 election did not cease upon successful passage of the Tillman Act. Parker's allegations led to the founding of the Publicity Law Organization of the State of New York (Pollock 1926, 10). This organization successfully secured the passage of the nation's first campaign publicity law and later developed into a national organization seeking similar reporting requirements for all federal candidates. Although Congress did not pass a law until 1910 requiring committees operating in two or more states to report any contributions or expenditures made in connection with campaigns for the House of Representatives, Overacker reported that the pressures of the publicity movement led both national party committees to publish accounts voluntarily of contributions in the 1908 election in compliance with New York's publicity law (Overacker 1932, 237).[4] Later amendments to the Publicity Act in 1911 established spending limits for federal campaigns; required House and Senate campaigns to report receipts and expenditures; mandated campaign committees to report their finances before and after primary and general elections, and limited House campaign spending to $5,000 (about $89,000 in 2000) and Senate spending to $10,000 (about $180,000 in 2000) or an amount set by state law, whichever was less (Corrado 1997). The Supreme Court later struck down the reporting requirements and primary expenditure limits in *Newberry v. United States* (256 U.S. 232, 1921).[5]

Campaign reform began anew after the Teapot Dome revelations in 1924. Interior Secretary Albert Fall was charged with leasing the Naval Oil Reserves located at Teapot Dome, Wyoming, to private businessmen. Further allegations contended that, in exchange for the leases, contributors donated to the Republican National Committee to clear its debt from the 1920 campaign (Overacker 1932, 148–149). Although the complete story behind the Teapot Dome scandal would not become known until the Senate's Walsh Committee renewed the investigation in 1928, public outcry pushed Congress to pass the Corrupt Practices Act of 1925.

Conforming to the *Newberry* decision, the Corrupt Practices Act removed all regulations concerning primary election finance. The disclosure rules now required all multi-state political committees as well as House and Senate candidates to file quarterly reports with the Clerk of the House listing all contributions of $100 or more (about $975 in 2000). Spending limits were also put into place: $25,000 for the Senate and $5,000 for the House (about $249,000 and $49,000, respectively, in 2000), unless state laws called for less. This act, with some amendments to the contribution limits to congressional candidates and the addition of expenditure limits for multi-state party committees made in 1940, governed federal elections until its replacement by the Federal Election Campaign Act of 1971.

The campaign finance reforms of the early twentieth century demonstrated the Progressive fear of concentrated power and the desire to expand participation in the political process. Banning corporate contributions prevented the outward appearance of corrupt elected officials; publicity of campaign contributions allowed public debate regarding the propriety of individual campaign contributions; and limiting campaign spending was seen as leveling the political playing field. The other democratic reforms established by the Progressives, such as the institution of primary elections, the direct election of U.S. senators, the adoption of the Australian ballot, and the extension of the franchise to women, flowed from the same philosophic underpinnings.

These early money reforms failed. The Corrupt Practices Act of 1925 contained several loopholes through which parties and candidates could drive armored truckloads of money. By limiting the scope of the reporting requirements to multi-state committees, money could evade regulation by operating in only one state. The act's expenditure limitations collapsed when candidates created more than one committee to conduct campaign business. By applying the limits to committees rather than each individual candidate for office, candidates and parties evaded the law by spawning several committees to fund their election activities. (This last loophole remained open until the Federal Election Campaign Act of 1971 required candidates to register one official committee as its campaign organization.) The regulations did little to stem the flow of money to political parties or candidates, and the minimal reporting requirements still meant large sums of money remained hidden from public scrutiny.

Progressive campaign finance regulations also neglected to address spending by noncandidate or nonparty organizations. The Tillman Act, rather than remove corporate influence from elections, merely shifted it from the corporation to individual businessmen. The centrifugal forces of primary campaigns, direct election of senators, increasing campaign costs, and the removal of a source of party finance undermined parties' control over the electoral process. Other independent forces beyond corporations, such as interest groups organized around specific issue concerns, began asserting their political will by entering election contests outside formal partisan channels.

One prominent participant in the new form of political activity was the Anti-Saloon League. Formed in the late 1890s in Oberlin, Ohio, the Anti-Saloon League employed campaign tactics familiar to students of modern interest group politics. The League intervened in congressional races, published voting records of candidates on the issue of prohibition, engaged in party platform discussions, submitted pledges to candidates, and lobbied incumbents on Capitol Hill to support legislation that prohibited the sale of intoxicating beverages (Kerr 1985: 192, 140; Odegard 1928: 88, 91). The power of the Anti-Saloon League frightened some politicians, and the League's track record convinced skeptics of their influence. "The average member of Congress," wrote Louis Seibold, "is more afraid of the Anti-Saloon League than he is even of the president of the United States. He does not hesitate to take issue with the chief executive of the country over important matters of state; but his courage vanishes into thin air when the whip of the Anti-Saloon League cracks a command" (quoted in Odegard 1928, 128). According to League lobbyist Wayne Wheeler, "We went into every congressional district where there was a chance to elect a dry and waged as strong a fight as candidates have ever seen" (quoted in Kerr 1985, 192). Political scientist Peter Odegard reported that even in the days shortly after the League's founding, it wielded extensive political clout: "In Ohio, between 1895 and 1903, over seventy members of the legislature, who were entitled by the custom of their parties to renomination but who had been antagonistic to the League's legislative program, were opposed and every one of them was defeated" (Odegard 1928, 97).

In 1926, Senator James Reed of Missouri launched an inquiry into the League's financial involvement in campaign activities, itself a sign of the League's perceived clout. The League cooperated in the investigation, but disputed whether or not it had to submit statements of its activities in accordance with the publicity acts of 1910 and 1911, as well as the more recently passed Corrupt Practices Act. The League maintained it did not fall under the provisions of the 1911 act as "the activities of the League are educational, scientific, and charitable rather than political as intended by the law" (Pollock 1926, 200). This distinction, between educational and political activity, became a frequent line of defense for interest groups involved in electioneering-style activities. Unions hewed to this same position in the 1950s when expenditures made from their general fund were under attack (see the Subcommittee on Privileges and Elections of the Committee on Rules and Administration 1956; hereafter referred to as the Gore Committee Hearings), and so did other interest groups and corporations engaging in independent expenditures nearly seventy years later.

THE NEW DEAL TO THE 1970s: THE POWER
OF LABOR AND THE COST OF CAMPAIGNS

Progressive reforms largely concerned the influence of business money in politics and the need for publicity. Developments from the 1930s to the 1970s changed the focus of campaign finance reform efforts. After the passage of the Wagner Act in 1935 and the success of Roosevelt's New Deal coalition, conservative forces became concerned with labor's new-found electoral strength (Corrado 1997, 30; Sousa 1999, 381). Unions had relatively little electoral impact before this time, but the appearance of the Non-Partisan League of the AFL and CIO worried conservatives. Corporate money, in the form of individual contributions by businessmen, most likely dwarfed the financial resources of the Non-Partisan League, but the two unions had contributed nearly $750,000 (equivalent to $9.1 million in 2000), mostly to Democrats, in the 1936 election (Sousa 1999: 381). With labor's emergence as a serious player in electoral politics, calls began for the curtailment of labor's authority and the extension of the Tillman ban on corporate contributions to labor. Conservatives temporarily accomplished this in 1943 with the Smith Connally Act (the War Disputes Act), which prohibited labor from using general treasury funds for contributions to political candidates. This act expired six months after the war, but was permanently extended in 1947 when Congress overrode President Truman's veto to pass the Taft-Hartley Act (the Labor Management Relations Act).

In 1939, the scope of the Pendleton Act was enlarged by the Hatch Act to include those federal workers not previously covered. The Hatch Act prohibited federal employees from engaging in political activity and specifically from soliciting political contributions. The legislation responded to the unprecedented expansion of the New Deal administrative state and fear that the Democratic majority would benefit from dispensing the spoils with a federal political machine (Corrado 1997, 30; Thayer 1973, 71). Amendments to the act in the succeeding year placed a $3 million spending limit on party committees operating in multiple states and a $5,000 annual limit on individual contributions to federal candidates, or about $36 million and $60,000, respectively, in 2000 (Corrado 1997, 30; Thayer 1973; Sorauf 1992, 7). Once again, the limits were easily evaded with multiple committees and contributions to state and local committees that did not fall under the act's jurisdiction.

In 1956, the Senate Subcommittee on Privileges and Elections, chaired by Senator Albert Gore, Sr., held a series of hearings addressing a mounting problem—the rising cost of campaigns. Testimony before the committee indicated that the federal nomination and election campaigns in 1952 cost about $140 million (equivalent to about $900 million in 2000), an increase of roughly 60 percent from 1940 (Gore Committee Hearings 1956, 10). The chairmen of the Democratic and Republican National Committees testified separately that the rising costs of campaigns were driven in large part by television. Between 1940 and 1956, television and radio advertising had become staples of modern campaigns, especially in presidential contests. DNC Chair Paul Butler called for free television time to "greatly reduce the dependence of political parties upon special interest contributors" (Gore Committee Hearings 1956: 14). According to figures provided by Alexander Heard, both party committees expended more than 30 percent of their national committee budget on television and radio in 1952 (Gore Committee Hearings 1956, 239).

The committee also was interested in the channels by which money flowed into politics. As the committee discovered, Taft-Hartley did not remove labor influence from politics any more than Tillman removed corporate influence. Testimony to the Gore Committee about union use of their general treasuries to fund so-called "educational" activities relied on the same defenses employed by the Anti-Saloon League concerning its electoral activities.[6] Other organizations took advantage of this distinction between the political and the educational, working around the spirit of the law by adhering to its letter. For example, Americans for Democratic Action defended their production of voter guides as educational despite their clearly partisan goal of electing Democrats (Gore Committee Hearings 1956, 283). Interests had become increasingly willing to work outside the parties and candidates to influence elections.[7]

THE FEDERAL ELECTION CAMPAIGN ACT OF 1971

The Federal Election Campaign Act (FECA) of 1971, the work of two years of deliberation, was the most significant and important change in the rules of campaign finance since the 1925 Corrupt Practices Act it was designed to replace. A review of the floor debates, committee reports, and *New York Times* articles from the era suggests that the rising cost of campaigns was lawmakers' central concern. Incumbent senators and representatives pushed reform to protect themselves from well-financed challengers. Kolodny suggests "the 1968 election was particularly important for motivating extensive reforms because of serious questions that arose regarding political advertising on television" (Kolodny 1998, 127). Witnesses at hearings held by the Senate Commerce Committee in 1969 noted that "many House races cost at least $100,000—of which 40 to 50 percent is often spent on broadcast time" (*Congressional Quarterly Weekly Report* 1969, 12).[8] The cost per vote in the presidential races had soared from 29 cents in 1960 to 60 cents in 1968 (*CQ* 1969, 12). In September 1970, the House passed HR 18434, limiting broadcast spending by candidates. The Senate had passed a similar bill earlier in the year, and both houses passed overwhelmingly the conference report (S3637).[9] President Nixon, however, vetoed the bill on October 12.

Congress again tackled the issue of campaign costs and restricting broadcast expenditures in March 1971. Senator Mike Gravel (D-Alaska), alarmed by political broadcasting costs of $59 million in 1968, cosponsored a bill calling for extensive free airtime for federal, state, and local candidates (CQ 1971a, 521). Republican Senators Hugh Scott of Pennsylvania and Charles Mathias of Maryland sponsored a bill providing for lower campaign advertising costs during the four weeks prior to the election. Their stated intent was "to shorten election campaigns by encouraging candidates to use time during the period immediately prior to elections rather than three or four months ahead" (CQ 1971b, 553). Senator Edmund Muskie (D-Maine) recommended that "media spending should be limited so that no candidate can overwhelm his opponent or the electorate with an advertising campaign of monumental cost, and in effect, buy his way into office" (CQ 1971b, 554). No mention was made of special interest media efforts.

Committee hearings and floor debate throughout the spring focused on the high cost of campaigns. By April, the Senate Commerce Committee unanimously reported Senate bill 382, which restricted spending on television and radio advertising to 5 cents per voter and placed a $5,000 cap on individual contributions. Further, the bill prohibited any campaign spending not authorized by the candidate—finally closing the loophole from the 1925 Corrupt Practices Act and the 1940 Hatch Act. Provisions added later limited the amount candidates could contribute to their own campaigns and strengthened regulations concerning public disclosure.

The bill received strong bipartisan support, winning a majority of both parties in both chambers. The measure may have received bipartisan support because it shielded incumbents; if anything, the bill disadvantaged Republican candidates as a whole because they did not hold the majority in either house. But if individual members were concerned with their own re-election first and party control second, the broad support of incumbents makes sense. The bill, as signed by Nixon, did not concern itself with the party's role in campaign financing or interest group campaigning. The congressional campaign committees "were still limited in operations, largely invisible to anyone off Capitol Hill" (Kolodny 1998, 127).[10]

FEDERAL ELECTION CAMPAIGN ACT: THE 1974 AMENDMENTS

Abuses by the 1972 Nixon campaign instigated the 1974 campaign reform drive. Unlike 1971, the debate was more concerned with corruption than it had been three years prior, harkening back to the discussion during the Progressive Era. The 1974 bill grew out of a failed measure advanced by Senator

Claibourne Pell (D-RI) in the previous Congress. As passed by the Senate Committee on Rules and Administration in February 1974, the bill capped candidate spending at 15 cents per voter or $175,000 for the Senate (whichever was greater) and at $90,000 for the House. Public financing would also be available via a check-off system, but candidates could choose how to fund their campaigns (choosing public, private, or a mix of the two) as long as they remained within the expenditure caps. In addition to candidate expenditure limitations, parties were restricted to spending no more than 2 cents per voter in general elections while individual donations were capped at $3,000 per candidate with an aggregate limit of $25,000 per year (*CQ* 1974, 629). Interest groups and organizations were limited to $1,000 in independent expenditures in each race and restrictions were placed on individual candidate contributions to their own campaigns.

For the first time, major provisions dealt with political parties and organized interests directly. The committee majority believed the bill would strengthen political parties (*CQ* 1974, 629). Presumably, the strengthening of parties was accomplished by restricting the financial activities of interest groups, providing public financing to candidates, and allotting a large financial role to the parties. The committee also saw the bill's public financing as a means to prevent corruption (U.S. Congress, Senate, Committee on Rules and Administration 1974, 4). Pell argued in defense of the 1974 bill, noting "we can, through enlightened legislative action, create a climate which minimizes the cause of abuse, and we can return to our voters their rights to choose candidates who are not beholden to the large, and so often compromising, political contribution" (U.S. Congress, Senate 1974, 4439).

As the Senate debate continued in the spring of 1974, the House Administration Committee held hearings on public financing. Here, the idea faced stiffer opposition. The chairman of the committee, Wayne Hays, opposed public financing for federal elections. Unlike the Senate bill, the House bill coming out of committee put less stringent restrictions on party contributions and independent expenditures by individuals and groups. The vote was unanimous, but the Republicans did offer a minority report suggesting the regulations would undermine the role of political parties in the American system:

> The minority strongly believes that the national and state committees of the major parties should be excluded from the definition of political committee for the purposes of contribution limitation. The national and state committees have been traditionally the policy-making bodies of the major parties and are cornerstones of our political system. The definition in the bill presently treats these important committees equally with all other committees, even small special interest committees. The national and state committees must be permitted the ability to assist candidates as the need arises so that a strong and dynamic party system can be maintained. (U.S. Congress, House 1974, 117)

The final version of FECA amendments signed into law by President Ford was stripped of its public funding provisions for Senate and House campaigns. Restrictions on expenditures by candidates personally and by their organizations were established, as well as individual contribution limits of $1,000 per candidate per race (capped at a yearly maximum of $25,000 to all federal candidates) and political action committee (PAC) contribution limits of $5,000 per candidate per race (with no yearly aggregate limits). Political action committees, a feature of the political landscape since the appearance of Labor's Non-Partisan League in the 1930s and COPE in the 1950s, were, for the first time, recognized explicitly by statute.[11] Party organizations were restricted to $5,000 in direct contributions to candidates. They could also spend an additional $10,000 "on behalf of" each House candidate and an additional $20,000 or 2 cents per eligible voter, whichever was greater, "on behalf of" a Senate candidate.[12] The spending limits placed upon House and Senate candidates, as well as national party spending on behalf of candidates, were indexed to inflation, but the contribution limits of $1,000 for individuals and $5,000 for PACs and organizations were not. The media limits imposed by the 1971 act were repealed. Candidates, parties, and PACs were required to report the names of their contributors. The bill also established a commission to oversee federal elections, implement provisions, and enforce the regulations of campaign financing.[13]

THE COURTS STEP IN: INTERPRETING FECA FROM 1976 TO 1996

The constitutionality of the FECA amendments was challenged immediately by Senator James Buckley of New York and former U.S. Senator George McGovern of South Dakota. As Congress had provided for expedited review in the legislation, the Court considered and handed down its decision a little more than a year after the FECA amendments became law. In *Buckley v. Valeo* (424 U.S. ___, 1976), the Court held all limits on expenditures to be unconstitutional violations of First Amendment rights, while upholding campaign contribution limits. They also found that the Federal Election Commission (FEC), the body constructed by Congress to oversee implementation of FECA, undermined the separation of power between the executive and legislative branches. Congress immediately acted to reconstitute the FEC to meet the court's objections, most notably making the commissioners presidential appointees.

Buckley seemed to boost interest group strength in the electoral process while diminishing the role of parties. Non-indexation of individual and PAC contribution limits would have shrunk the volume of money parties could marshal in support of their candidates in any event, but the Supreme Court struck the sharper blow. The candidate spending limits imposed by Congress in 1974 would have restricted the flow of individual and special interest contributions to candidates, preventing party assistance to candidates from being swamped by funds from these other sources. Its rejection of limits on candidate spending created strong incentives for candidates to build prodigious fundraising machines that did not rely on the generosity of the party. For candidates, the pool of party money might well seem insignificant in comparison to the money offered by individual donors and political action committees.[14]

Another important facet of the *Buckley* decision was the distinction made by the Court between express advocacy and political speech more generally. The Court suggested that if groups did not engage in campaign activities or advertising containing "explicit words of advocacy of election or defeat" they would be free to spend as they wished. The distinction between educational and political advertising, established in practice by the Anti-Saloon League in the 1920s and aggressively expanded by labor post-Taft-Hartley, had received the Court's legal sanction. Although FECA paved the path for legitimate special interest assistance to the candidate directly via PACs, the Court gave its tacit consent to interest group activity external to parties and candidates that was political but not expressly seeking the election or defeat of a candidate. In a series of court cases since *Buckley*, the courts have further defined and expanded the ability of interest groups to independently spend money on these controversial issue ads.[15]

The role of special interests in the electoral process, legitimized by the legislative endorsement of the legality of PACs in 1974, was enhanced by the FEC's ruling regarding the funding of PACs. In 1975, the FEC ruled that corporations and unions could pay directly from their treasuries for the overhead costs of their political action committees (the SUN PAC advisory opinion).[16] This decision, according to Frank Sorauf, "removed the final impediment to the race of groups to organize PACs and enter electoral politics" (Sorauf 1997). The decision encouraged corporate interests to establish PACs, something they had been largely reluctant to do despite labor's introduction of PACs in the 1940s.

Congress again reformed the campaign finance system in 1976 and 1979 with amendments to FECA. The 1976 amendments largely concerned the reconstitution of the FEC to meet the Supreme Court's objections in *Buckley*, but it also revised some of the contribution limits established by the 1974 act—most notably allowing the national party committee and the party senatorial committee to contribute a combined $17,500 to individual Senate candidates and restricting individual contributions at $5,000 to PACs and $20,000 to political parties. PACs were also limited to giving no more than $15,000 to political parties in direct contributions.

As noted previously, Republicans in 1974 were concerned about the impact the new regulations would have on political parties. Fearful that local and state parties were disadvantaged by the new rules, Congress sought protection of their role by allowing them to raise and spend unlimited sums on get-out-the-vote drives, voter registration activities, and other "party building" efforts (Corrado 1996). Through what would become known as "soft money" (in contrast to "hard money" contributions intended specifically to assist candidates), individuals, corporations, labor unions, and other organizations could now give money directly from their treasuries to fund party building activities. Congress had now legitimized another avenue by which private interests could influence the process; unlike the issue advocacy ads allowed by *Buckley*, this avenue funneled money from interest groups through parties to candidates. The ability of interest groups to engage in issue ads independently had shifted control of the electoral process away from candidates and parties; the 1979 soft money loophole seemed to tip the balance toward parity between the parties and interest groups potentially at the expense of candidates. Exactly how "soft money" would operate was not fully defined in the 1979 amendments, but the amendments legitimized this form of expenditure. Later, decisions by the FEC would clarify specifically what was and was not permissible under the rubric of soft money.

Most importantly, in 1995, the FEC ruled that the parties could spend soft money dollars to run "issue ads." These ads were clearly intended to affect election outcomes but avoided the use of "magic words" such as "vote for" and "vote against." The ads could be run regardless of the wishes of the candidate purportedly helped by the ad. As the national parties spent unlimited funds on what were effectively campaign advertisements, the parties' demand for soft money dollars grew tremendously along with concerns about the propriety of such funding. Private interests constantly tapped for additional funds, including the chief executive officers of Fortune 500 corporations, eventually would complain that the parties' requests for funds were incessant and intimidating.

The most important court case arising from FECA regulations after *Buckley* in 1976 was the Court's 1996 ruling in *Colorado Republican Federal Campaign Committee v. Federal Election Commission* (518 U.S. 604, 1996). This landmark decision allowed political parties to engage directly in independent expenditures and express advocacy ads. While parties had previously been able to spend soft money on issue advocacy, the Court decided that they could also engage in express advocacy so long as it was done so independently of candidates and paid for by federal "hard" dollars. Unlike the amounts parties could contribute to candidates, or could spend in coordination with candidates,[17] these independent expenditures would not be limited. Parties, independent of candidates, could spend what they wished to assist the candidate. Control of the election process shifted somewhat toward parties and special interests, while candidates lost some control of their own electoral destinies. This sense that candidates had lost control of campaigns, along with an outcry about the vast sums being raised in soft money, resonated loudly in the ultimately successful legislative efforts after the mid-1990s to restrict the ability of interests to conduct issue advocacy during the election season and to restrict the soft money being collected by political parties. Candidates were pushing back against a system leaning increasingly toward the parties and interests.

Cycles, Trends, and Themes in the Party-Group-Candidate Money Relationship

History is not "simply one damn thing after another," as has sometimes been asserted. Our brief overview of campaign finance reform in the United States over the past 150 years demonstrates that certain patterns recur, suggesting more than a simple linear progression of events. Indeed, we believe that four consistent themes can be teased out of the historical sequence: First, reforms follow perceived corruption or scandals in the electoral process; second, significant expansion or contraction of the national state is a critical catalyst for campaign finance abuses and reforms; third, there has been an increasing willingness by private interests to use independent means to influence the electoral process; and fourth, the relative strength of parties, groups, and candidates in the electoral process depends on the need for resources and on the scale of mobilization deemed necessary for victory. These four themes lend a better understanding both to the institutional reform efforts of the past and the likely effect of such efforts in the present and near future on the party-group-candidate money nexus.

Reforms Follow Perceived Corruption

No doubt the most obvious pattern is that each of the most significant reform moments of the past one hundred years—the Progressive Era, the 1970s, and the early twenty-first century—followed crises of legitimacy for that system.[18] The perception that private money had lined the parties' pockets in the late nineteenth century and the abuses in the 1904 election led to the demands for reform in the first decade of the twentieth century. Large donations received by the Nixon campaign helped spark the reforms of the early 1970s. Perceptions that soft money contributions corrupted the policy process pushed along the reform effort at the end of the 1990s. And the very fact that elections were becoming more expensive was itself converted into a corruption-prevention argument: At least part of the concern with expensive campaigns was the dependent relationship they might foster between private interests with funds and candidates, along with their parties, in need of those funds.

To be sure, corruption or perceived abuses were not the only galvanizing factors behind reforms, but these prominent scandals provided a public advertisement for campaign finance reform that encouraged some legislators to endorse reforms they might not otherwise have rushed to support. Congressional investigations of both major parties' fundraising practices during the 1996 presidential campaign, and the financial improprieties involving the Enron corporation, for example, provided publicity weapons that would prove valuable to political entrepreneurs such as Senators John McCain and Russell Feingold.

If campaign finance abuse might be said to be a necessary condition for significant reform in the party-group money relationship, it is not a sufficient condition. After all, major reform periods followed a long stretch of complaints about finance and an equally long stretch in which politicians did nothing to address the problem. It is clear enough, then, that corruption does not automatically self-correct and produce a set of reforms that eliminate abuses.

SIGNIFICANT STATE EXPANSION OR CONTRACTION CATALYZES MONEY ABUSES AND REFORMS

In his analysis of cycles of political culture in the United States, Samuel Huntington (1981) suggests that Americans grapple continuously with the gap between their institutions and their ideals. How Americans resolve this gap at different times, he suggests, can be described as cynicism (tolerate the gap), complacency (ignore the gap), hypocrisy (deny the gap), or moralism (eliminate the gap). If Americans do indeed often perceive that their institutions do not honor their ideals, why is it that Americans only rarely reach a point of moralism and reform? Similarly, we noted in our first theme previously that there is a ready supply of questionable behavior or outright abuse in campaign finance, but those abuses do not always translate into reforms. At certain historical points, however, the perceived gravity of corruption sparks a movement for reform. Why?

We suggest that the perceived gravity of campaign finance abuses, of the mismatch between institutions and ideals, will be more severe when there is a significant expansion or contraction of national state activity. Consider first government expansion. As the role of government in society and economy expands, the umbrella of federal control over private activity broadens. To simplify, private interests respond to this expansion in one of two ways: They seek to capitalize on the expansion of federal services and rules, or they seek ways to get out from under the yoke of federal control, perhaps by selling services and goods to government, perhaps by disadvantaging competitors in the marketplace. Whether they see expanding federal control and power as a threat or an opportunity, these interests have a genuine reason to want to win friends in high federal places. Campaign contributions or assistance is one means to accomplish that. Significant expansions in the state encourage new political activity by private interests, and sometimes this activity may cross the border of "acceptable" behavior. The explosion of federal regulation in the early twentieth century and the vast expansion of social and regulatory programs in the 1960s and early 1970s encouraged political activity by private interests (see Budde 1980; Gais 1996). The expansion of the bureaucracy during the 1930s led to fears that government officials would not only influence other members of the bureaucracy, but could effectively hold private interests hostage at the behest of benefactors such as labor unions. Campaign finance reform was passed in each of these periods to address the perception that private interests were gaining a strong grip on the national polity. The irony, of course, is that a good portion of this private action was a *reaction* to policy actions in the national polity itself.

Consider next government contraction. The 1990s may not have produced the revolution in government scope hoped for by Republicans after the 1994 election, but the decade was notable for contraction in a variety of programs and services. Just as with government growth, retrenchment in government programs and services or changes in regulatory rules invite private pressure on government to shape these developments in particular ways. In the 1970s, private pressure took the form of political action committee contributions; in the 1990s, this action increasingly took the form of soft money contributions. Neither was illegal, but both generated dismay about the prevalence of private money in elections.

Aside from generating demands among affected interests, periods of significant state expansion or contraction can also affect public perceptions of the political process. In particular, as new expansionist or contractionist policies emerge, citizens gain a sense of the relative power of competing social forces in the U.S.—and if they do not gain this sense themselves, there will be interest group activists who will tell them. Citizens will hear about the conflict between broad and narrow interests and, precisely because government is doing so much, the argument that narrow interests are benefiting at the expense of the public good will have some heft. Precisely because government is doing so much to grow or shrink the state, and interests are doing so much to get parties and candidates to listen, the gap between institutions and ideals may newly appear, to many citizens, to be unacceptably large.

INTERESTS INCREASINGLY TURN TO INDEPENDENT POLITICAL ACTION

These first two historical tendencies are somewhat cyclical or episodic, but the growth of independent action by interests has been more secular in nature. Over time, interests increasingly have been able to influence the electoral environment independent of candidates and political parties. This process seems to have relatively little to do with law and much to do with political learning. That is, interests have experimented with new forms of participation and, facing no legal sanctions, these new forms spread. Between the turn of the century and the 1940s, interests participated most often through the political parties in the form of individual contributions by wealthy donors (corporations and unions were prohibited from contributing to federal candidates). Beginning in the 1940s, labor became an increasingly important force in Democratic party politics, and although labor nearly always assisted Democratic candidates, much of labor's activity was determined by its own political calculations rather than the party's calculations. Labor's success in motivating workers with get-out-the-vote drives and informational campaigns would prove to be a model followed by other groups, particularly those appealing to conservative Christians. Although unable to contribute labor union funds to the parties or candidates, labor and its imitators found independent means to influence election results on a party's behalf.

Labor was also an early player in political action committees, along with some industrial organizations and professional associations. Again, other groups were slow to pick up on this model until PACs were explicitly recognized in the reform legislation of the 1970s. With the PAC model now embraced by law, a flood of interests sought to develop this form of influence in the election process. But PACs were tied to parties and candidates—PACs could obviously make independent decisions about whom to support, but the money was given over to candidates and parties rather than spent by the interests themselves.

This next level of independence, campaign spending that remained in control of the interest, was facilitated by independent expenditures. Again, some experimenting and pushing the legal envelope led to an embrace of independent expenditures by the Supreme Court. Whether in the form of express advocacy or issue advocacy, independent expenditures allowed interests direct involvement in the art and science of election persuasion, often to the dismay of candidates and their parties.

As far as we can discern, none of these activities was prohibited at any time following the Progressive Era. In theory, PACs, private persuasion efforts, and independent expenditures were every bit as legal in the 1920s as in the 1990s. Soft money contributions to political parties were, similarly, the result of experimentation. Although soft money contributions do not afford the same level of independence as independent expenditures, they allow corporations and unions to engage in activity that is remarkably close to activity specifically prohibited by federal law. What changed over time was not so much law as practice, with private interests playing entrepreneurial roles in discovering new and independent ways to advance their programs in the electoral process.

PARTY AND GROUP ELECTORAL STRENGTH DEPENDS ON PARTIES' NEEDS FOR RESOURCES AND THE SCALE OF MOBILIZATION PERCEIVED NECESSARY FOR VICTORY

Political machines created during the mid-nineteenth century contended with a relatively small voting universe. Because the voting universe was small, minimum winning coalitions were also not very large and were easily maintained by expending such resources as patronage positions and social services for newly-arrived immigrants. As the potential voting universe expanded through increased suffrage and a liberalization of registration laws, successful machines were able to expand their revenue base by increasing taxes on the middle class or annexing additional lands to increase the tax base, producing the financial resources necessary to incorporate the new voters into the winning coalition. Machines that either could not expand their resource base to incorporate these new voters, or alternatively, failed to prevent the expansion of suffrage to these new elements, collapsed upon their own weight.

Steven Erie (1988) paints the problem facing nineteenth and twentieth-century political bosses as one of obtaining sufficient resources to build and maintain a minimum winning coalition in the face of an increasingly open political process. Erie's approach informs our understanding of the relationship between parties, groups, candidates, and money. Parties, interest groups, and candidates need to mobilize resources in order to win elections. The relationship between candidates, political parties, and interest groups cannot be understood, however, merely as a function of the openness of the political process. Erie's model assumes that an expanded voting universe, such as that faced by political machines during the wave of suffrage expansion in the 1830s and the wave in the 1920s, leads to increased resource needs because there are more voters to mobilize into electoral coalitions. Mass mobilization, however, is not a prerequisite for victory at the polls. Assuming a two-party race, one needs only a majority of people choosing to vote on election day. If many voters can and do participate, then mass mobilization efforts are required by parties and candidates. If few voters are able to participate, or alternatively, few choose to, then mass mobilization is not a prerequisite for victory. What truly drives the resource need equation, then, is whether or not mass mobilization efforts are required to achieve victory.

Efforts to mass mobilize may require substantial resources, but these efforts can benefit from economies of scale and from high degrees of certainty about the targets of resource deployment. When faced with an expanded electorate that participates less, however, the costs of mobilization can increase along with the uncertainty of resource deployment. When the target audience is the total audience, a strategy of doing as much as possible and getting it in front of as many eyes as possible makes sense. When the target is but a slice of the whole, calculations become more complicated. Individual voters must be targeted and appealed to based upon their personal interests and motivations. This invariably increases communication costs as economies of scale are lost. It also increases uncertainty: Which voters should be targeted? What appeals will be effective and to which voters? Because it is not certain who in this large pool of potential participants will in fact decide to participate, parties and candidates may perceive a need for substantial resources.

The ease and certainty by which parties and candidates mobilize these resources intimately affects their mutual relationship. It also determines the power of interest groups in the electoral process. If parties and candidates have funding mechanisms they independently control that provide them with their resource needs, the ability of interests to affect the process is minimal. If, however, parties and candidates require resources that outstrip their funding apparatus, then interest groups are empowered relative to parties and candidates.

By examining at any given point in time the ability of parties to provide the electoral resources they and their candidates require, and the necessity of mass mobilization for electoral victory, we can develop scenarios suggesting how interest groups and political parties might be advantaged or disadvantaged in the electoral process. These scenarios are presented in Table 7.1.[19]

1860s–1890s In the mid-nineteenth century, parties dominated politics. Controlling both the nomination process and the production of ballots, parties held the key to elected office. The price for the key typically took the form of party loyalty and forfeiting a portion of one's salary to fund the armies of voters and poll watchers necessary to maintain electoral coalitions. The official machinery of government was employed to cement political loyalties further. Patronage and a host of social services were provided at the municipal level in exchange for support on Election Day. The ability of the party to create winning electoral coalitions and maintain them with the official machinery of the state allowed them financial self-sufficiency. As a result, the need to gather electoral resources outside the state apparatus or party-loyal, patronage-holding local and state officials was low. Political participation was high and widespread, so mass mobilization efforts were required to win elections. Parties and their local machines were well-suited to

TABLE 7.1   THE NEED FOR VOTES AND MONEY
AS THE CORE OF THE PARTY, GROUP, CANDIDATE RELATIONSHIP

	STATUS OF PARTY'S RESOURCE NEEDS	
RELATIONSHIP BETWEEN VOTES AND VICTORY	*NEEDS MET*	*NEEDS UNMET*
High need for mass mobilization	Individual candidates weak Interest groups typically blackmailed Party strength high *1860s–1890s*	Individual candidates weak Interest groups utilize party electoral strategies Party strength high *1890s–1950s*
Low need for mass mobilization	Individual candidates and parties on more equal footing Interest groups balance party and candidate access strategies Interest group parity with parties *1980s–present*	Individual candidates strong Interest groups engage in candidate access strategies Parties weak *1960s–1970s*

provide both the manpower and money to fund these activities with money from the state (Yearley 1970). In a system of self-perpetuating party power and finance, interest groups were disadvantaged in their efforts to engage in electoral politics. Party politicians typically utilized their positions of power to extract resources from interest groups not for electoral purposes, but to enhance their personal wealth.

1890s–1950s   The Pendleton Act's passage in 1882 put the funding of the party machine in doubt. No longer able to rely as heavily upon the state to fund mass-based politics, parties had to turn to another source for money. At first, this source was big business. Later, it became individuals and labor, as well as other assorted interest groups. The lack of financial security for political parties and candidates gave interest groups more political influence than they held in the earlier part of the nineteenth century, and that need grew as the advertising style in campaigns became the dominant mode of campaigning during this period (McGerr 1986).

Political coalition building still required mass mobilization of voters, however, and interest groups were ill-suited to engage in politics of this type by themselves. Voting rates, though lower than the mid- and late-nineteenth century, were still high, and female suffrage expanded the voting universe. Some interest groups such as the Anti-Saloon League engaged in political activities affecting individual elections, but much of their power and influence still had to be channeled through the political party.

1960s–1970s The era of mass-mobilized politics did not last forever. After the 1890s, parties were under siege. They could no longer sufficiently finance their activities; they no longer controlled the nomination process; and the erosion of patronage hurt the party's ability to mobilize voters and maintain secure electoral coalitions for their candidates. To make matters worse, the boom in radio and television broadcasting allowed for communication to occur directly between the candidate and voters, and even interest groups and voters.

These conditions led to the development of a more candidate-centered politics. Both the need for resources and the parties' ability to fund their candidates were affected. Candidates needed substantial sums to finance their individualistic appeals to the populace, and they built organizations that were well-suited to raise the sums necessary without extensive help from the parties. With fewer voters participating, and with those who did vote identifying less with either political party, the mass-based mobilization efforts of parties became less relevant to political success. Parties had become weak and individual candidates strong. In this situation, resource-needy candidates sought interest group money to fund their campaign efforts. The legitimatization of special interests by FECA encouraged interest groups to become more involved in electoral politics, as did the FEC's favorable decision regarding corporate and union monies funding PAC overhead costs. Special interest groups began to form PACs in substantial numbers and became a major source of money for individual candidates. In a time when it mattered less to get everyone to the polls and more to get select groups activated, interest groups, with their funds and their established means for reaching specialized constituencies, flourished in the electoral process.

1980s–Present The 1974 reforms and their subsequent interpretation by the courts ultimately shifted the balance between interest groups and parties. At first, parties seemed disadvantaged by the limits on what they could contribute to and spend on behalf of their candidates, but their position would improve over time. Individual and PAC contribution constraints put candidates in nearly full-time fundraising mode. PACs found that they faced a blizzard of funding requests from candidates, but most PACs were shoestring operations that did not have the political expertise to know where best to deploy their funds. Ironically, the very demand for PAC funds that arose from the candidate-centered campaign provided an opening for a new role for parties (Kayden 1980: 276). According to Herrnson, FECA "allowed the [Congressional campaign committees] to become major brokers with the PAC community and devote staff and resources exclusively to the purpose of matching PACs with appropriate candidates for their donations" (quoted in Kolodny 1998, 132). Candidates realized that even if parties were not necessarily providing the funds, parties played a critical role in directing PAC funds toward their campaigns. And parties of course could contribute directly to candidates as well.

Interest groups, whose heyday had been in the 1960s and 1970s, now had to operate through both the party and the candidate to become an electoral force. The advent of soft money merely replicated this pattern at a much higher scale, because now interests could donate hundreds of thousands of dollars directly to the parties, which the parties could then, for all practical purposes, deploy on behalf of specific candidates through issue advocacy and independent expenditures. Candidate dependence on parties and interests grew, though candidates still certainly did substantial fundraising on their own via individual contributions. Parties needed soft money to fund their new efforts, while interests needed to donate ever larger sums to be noticed in the ocean of soft money. Interest groups and political parties had reached a rough parity in campaign finance by the mid-1980s, and this parity continues at the onset of the twenty-first century.

CONCLUSION

Reform is difficult. Reforms attempting to channel the flow of money have met with the ingenuity of candidates, parties, and interests seeking to provide the electoral resources necessary to win. The most egregious examples of this behavior seem to occur during periods of significant state expansion or contraction. The evasion of the spirit if not letter of the law, however, is also the product of political learning. Labor's development of the PAC in the 1930s and 1940s, for example, was not against the law, but can be seen as circumventing the spirit of the law by providing a continuous flow of financial resources to candidates and parties.

Reforming money in politics is a problem of both supply and demand. Nearly every campaign reform effort in the past has dealt with the supply side of the equation: Tillman eliminated corporate contributions, Taft-Hartley labor money, and FECA constrained individual donors and parties. Each of these efforts restricted some form of money supply from entering the political process directly, and yet, those sources found some way of entering the process. Labor money funded "educational" campaigns, while corporations and wealthy individuals made soft money contributions.

Addressing the demand side of the equation has proved even more intractable. Reformers have attempted to deal with resource demand directly, most notably in the original version of FECA in 1971 and its subsequent amendments in 1974. In 1971, Congress implemented media expenditure restrictions and in 1974, spending limits indexed to inflation were imposed. The first were eliminated by the 1974 reforms; the second were overturned by the Supreme Court in *Buckley*. The difficulty has been in developing a system of reforms that limits the demand for money in a manner with which both the reformers and the Court can live.

Reforming money in politics is also a problem of self-interest: Reformers have very rarely enacted a reform that hurt their electoral fortunes. Consider the demand-side reforms—limits on media advertising, on overall campaign spending, and on expenditure of personal funds. What impact would these have had on congressional reformers? Those who passed the law were already in Congress—of course, this will always be the case—and many of them feared wealthy candidates spending enormous sums of money to unseat them. Similarly, since challengers typically need a large sum of money to compensate for the name recognition and other advantages of the incumbent, one might see "leveling the financial playing field" as an act of incumbent protection. These reforms might address the demand for money, but they might also arguably undermine the competitiveness of elections.

All this is not to say that reform should not be attempted in the future, but rather that those who have not learned the lessons and patterns of the past do truly seem destined to repeat them. The Bipartisan Campaign Reform Act (BCRA) signed into law in 2002 is a case in point. Proponents expect that banning issue advocacy advertisements sixty days prior to a general election (thirty days prior to a primary election), in combination with prohibiting soft money contributions to federal party committees, will curtail severely special interest influence in elections. But with parties financially weakened nationally, interest group resources will become even more prominent. Because campaigns still require significant resources targeted to segments of the electorate (rather than mass mobilization), candidates will turn increasingly to PAC and individual campaign donations to fill the party gap. Furthermore, efforts by special interests might simply shift from the national to state and local arenas—safe havens from federal campaign finance laws. Lastly, rather than reducing their electoral involvement, interests might simply shift their independent electoral action from issue advocacy to express advocacy.

To succeed, future reform must be institutionally aware, understanding how electoral contexts create and constrain the efforts of political actors engaging in campaigns *relative* to each other. It must also grapple with both the supply and demand side of the resource equation. Moreover, reform must recognize constitutional limitations as defined by the courts. The BCRA falls short by these measures. As we indicated previously, the institutional interplay between parties, groups, and candidates may lead to increasing the prominence of interests, despite the intent of the law's proponents to do precisely the opposite. Second, the law constrains supply but ignores demand. Lastly, the Court may well play the spoiler again, overturning parts of the law, with the ban on issue advocacy ads being perhaps the most vulnerable to rejection.

In reviewing the history of campaign finance reform, we have explained how the rules structuring the campaign finance system can determine the relationship between parties, candidates, and interests. Campaign finance laws, in combination with the relative need for mass mobilization, shape the electoral relationships between parties, interests, and candidates by determining whether electoral politics can be adequately funded by parties or candidates alone. The expansion and contraction of state capacity shakes the existing electoral system by pushing private interests into electioneering activities to protect their interests. This scramble for resources produces opportunities for candidates and parties to capitalize on the uncertainty facing private interests, creating the possibility of campaign finance abuses, which may then lead to calls for a restructuring of the campaign finance system. The campaign finance regime established under the new reforms changes the relationships governing interests, parties, and candidates. These relationships, as we have shown, are dynamic and, we would suggest, predictable. They also are diverse. As we have demonstrated, party and group electoral strength may well be inverse—when one is weak, the other is strong—but this need not be the case. Parity among parties, groups, and candidates is also possible. The task for reformers is to decide which of these diverse possibilities is best for democratic linkage and governance.

REFERENCES

Austin v. Michigan State Chamber of Commerce (494 U.S. 652, 1990).

Budde, Bernadette A. "Business Political Action Committees." In *Parties, Interest Groups, and Campaign Finance Laws.* Ed. Michael J. Malbin. Washington, D.C.: American Enterprise Institute, 1980.

Callow, Alexander B., Jr. *The Tweed Ring.* London: Oxford University Press, 1965.

Colorado Republican Federal Campaign Committee v. Federal Election Commission (518 U.S. 604, 1996)

Congressional Quarterly. "Ways Sought to Cope with Rising TV Campaign Costs." *Congressional Quarterly Weekly Report* (28 October 1969).

Congressional Quarterly. "Campaign Financing: The Senate Commerce Subcommittee." *Congressional Quarterly Weekly Report* (5 March 1971a).

Congressional Quarterly. "Campaign Financing: Witnesses Propose Alternatives." *Congressional Quarterly Weekly Report* (12 March 1971b).

Congressional Quarterly. "Campaign Financing Reform." *Congressional Quarterly Weekly Report* (9 March 1974).

Corrado, Anthony. "Money and Politics: A History of Federal Campaign Finance Law." In *Campaign Finance Reform: A Sourcebook.* Ed. Anthony Corrado, Thomas E. Mann, Daniel R. Ortiz, Trevor Potter, and Frank J. Sorauf. Washington: Brookings Institution Press, 1997.

Croly, Herbert D. *Marcus Alonzo Hanna: His Life and Work.* New York: The Macmillan Company, 1912.

Erie, Steven. *Rainbow's End: Irish-Americans and the Dilemmas of Urban Machine Politics, 1840–1985.* Berkeley: University of California Press, 1988.

FEC v. Colorado Republican Federal Campaign Committee (533 U.S. 431, 2001).

FEC v. Massachusetts Citizens for Life, Inc. (470 U.S. 238, 1986).

Gais, Thomas. *Improper Influence: Campaign Finance Law, Political Interest Groups, and Problem of Equality.* Ann Arbor: University of Michigan Press, 1996.

Griffith, Ernest S. *A History of American City Government: The Conspicuous Failure, 1870–1900.* New York: Praeger, 1974.

Hershkowitz, Leo. *Tweed's New York: Another Look.* Garden City: Anchor Books, 1978.

Hofstadter, Richard. *The Age of Reform: From Bryan to F.D.R.* New York: Vintage Books, 1955.

Huntington, Samuel P. *American Politics: The Promise of Disharmony.* Cambridge: Harvard University Press, 1981.

Kerr, K. Austin. *Organized for Prohibition: A New History of the Anti-Saloon League.* New Haven: Yale University Press, 1985.

Kayden, Xandra. "The Nationalization of the Party System." In *Parties, Interest Groups, and Campaign Finance Laws.* Ed. Michael J. Malbin. Washington, D.C.: American Enterprise Institute, 1980.

Kolodny, Robin. *Pursuing Majorities: Congressional Campaign Committees in American Politics.* Norman, OK: University of Oklahoma Press, 1998.

McGerr, Michael E. *The Decline of Popular Politics: The American North, 1865–1928.* New York: Oxford University Press, 1986.

Merton, Robert K. "The Latent Functions of the Machine." In *Urban Bosses, Machines, and Progressive Reformers.* Ed. Bruce M. Stave. Lexington: D.C. Heath and Company, 1972.

Miller, Nathan. *Theodore Roosevelt: A Life.* New York: Quill, 1992.

Miller, Stephen. *Special Interest Groups in American Politics.* New Brunswick: Transaction Books, 1983.

Mutch, Robert E. *Campaigns, Congress, and Courts.* New York: Praeger, 1988.

Odegard, Peter H. *Pressure Politics: The Story of the Anti-Saloon League.* New York: Columbia University Press, 1928.

Overacker, Louise. *Money in Elections.* New York: Macmillan Company, 1932.

Pollock, James K., Jr. *Party Campaign Funds.* New York: Alfred A. Knopf, 1926.

Potter, Trevor. "Issue Advocacy and Express Advocacy." In *Campaign Finance Reform: A Sourcebook.* Ed. Anthony Corrado, Thomas E. Mann, Daniel R. Ortiz, Trevor Potter, and Frank J. Sorauf. Washington: Brookings Institution Press, 1997.

Richardson, Jeremy. "The Market for Political Activism: Interest Groups as a Challenger to Political Parties." *West European Politics* 18, no. 1 (1995): 116–139.

Rodgers, Daniel T. *Contested Truths: Keywords in American Politics Since Independence.* Cambridge: Harvard University Press, 1987.

Schattschneider, E. E. *Semi-Sovereign People.* New York: Holt, Rinehart, and Winston, 1960.

Schiesl, Martin J. *The Politics of Efficiency: Municipal Administration and Reform in America, 1880–1920.* Berkeley: University of California Press, 1977.

Sorauf, Frank J. *Inside Campaign Finance: Myths and Realities.* New Haven: Yale University Press, 1992.

Sorauf, Frank J. "Political Action Committees." In *Campaign Finance Reform: A Sourcebook.* Ed. Anthony Corrado, Thomas E. Mann, Daniel R. Ortiz, Trevor Potter, and Frank J. Sorauf. Washington: Brookings Institution Press, 1997.

Sousa, David J. "No Balance in the Equities: Union Power in the Making and Unmaking of the Campaign Finance Regime." *Studies in American Political Development* 13, no. 3 (1999): 374–401.

Thayer, George. *Who Shakes the Money Tree?: American Campaign Financing Practices from 1789 to the Present.* New York: Simon & Schuster, 1973.

U.S. Congress. House. Committee on House Administration. *Federal Election Campaign Act Amendments of 1974: Report of the Committee on House Administration to Accompany H.R. 16090.* 93rd Congress, 2nd session, 1974.

U.S. Congress. Senate. *Senator Clairbourne Pell of Rhode Island Speaking for the Federal Election Campaign Act Amendments of 1974. S3044.* 93rd Congress, 2nd session. *Congressional Record* (26 March 1974).

U.S. Congress. Senate. Committee on Rules and Administration. *Federal Election Campaign Act Amendments of 1974: Report of the Committee on Rules and Administration to Accompany S3044.* 93rd Congress, 2nd session, 1974.

U.S. Congress. Senate. Subcommittee of the Committee on Privileges and Elections. *Campaign Contributions: Testimony before a Subcommittee of the Committee on Privileges and Elections.* 62nd Congress, 3rd session, 1912. (The Clapp Committee.)

U.S. Congress. Senate. Subcommittee on Privileges and Elections of the Committee on Rules and Administration. *1956 Presidential and Senatorial Campaign Contributions and Practices: Hearings before the Subcommittee on Privileges and Elections of the Committee on Rules and Administration.* 84th Congress, 2nd session, 1956. (The Gore Committee Hearings.)

United States v. Classic (313 U.S. 299, 1941).

Yearley, Clifton K. 1970. *The Money Machines: The Breakdown and Reform of Governmental and Party Finance in the North, 1860–1920.* Albany: State University of New York Press, 1970.

NOTES

1. Some historians paint the political machine in a more sympathetic light. Leo Hershkowitz suggests that the embittered publisher of the *New York Times* had been denied machine largesse, and thus began a public campaign to demonize Tweed (see Hershkowitz 1978). More broadly, Robert Merton maintains that political machines performed an important societal function by providing city services that outmoded municipal governments were unable to supply (Merton 1972).

2. States began limiting campaign contributions by corporations in the 1890s.

3. According to Hanna's biographer, Herbert Croly: "In the case of the banks, a regular assessment was levied, calculated, I believe, at the rate of one-quarter of one percent of their capital, and this assessment was for the most part paid. It is a matter of public record that large financial institutions such as the life insurance companies, were liberal contributors" (Croly 1912: 220).

4. Both national party committees were headquartered in New York City during this period.

5. The Court ruled that Congress could not regulate primary elections as these were within the purview of the states and the parties. This ruling was overturned nearly twenty years later when the Court allowed Congress to regulate primaries when they were an integral part of the general election process. See *United States v. Classic* (313 U.S. 299, 1941).

6. The co-directors of Labor's COPE (Committee on Political Education) asserted that "Our committee is a nonpartisan organization. Our purpose is to keep our members informed of these issues we have outlined here and of their ramifications as they extend down from the level of national policy to the home of the individual citizen. . . . We are not interested in the formation of a third party nor are we interested in becoming the appendage of any existing party. We have no desire to capture any party nor any ambition to attain personal political power" (Gore Committee Hearings 1956: 47).

7. A report commissioned by President Kennedy and published as the President's Commission on Campaign Costs in 1962 echoed many of the same concerns regarding the spiraling costs of elections. The committee did not denounce the insertion of money in the electoral process but, instead, recognized the need for money and recommended ways in which it could be generated while still protecting the system's integrity.

8. Rather than convert each of the dollar figures from the 1970s, we provide the following rule of thumb for interested readers: Dollar figures from 1971 should be multiplied by about 4.3 to obtain the equivalent amount of 2000 dollars; figures from 1974 should be multiplied by 3.7; and figures from 1979 should be multiplied by 2.5.

9. The measure passed the House by a vote of 247-111, and the Senate by 60–19.

10. The congressional campaign committees are the Democratic Congressional Campaign Committee, National Republican Congressional Committee, Democratic Senatorial Campaign Committee, and National Republican Senatorial Committee. These committees raise and disburse funds for their party's candidates; House candidates for the first two committees, Senate candidates for the latter two.

11. PACs are the campaign finance arm of corporations, unions, and groups but are legally separate from these organizations. A corporation cannot directly contribute to a House candidate, for example, but the corporation can establish a PAC, and that PAC can contribute.

12. This "on behalf of" spending would later become known as "coordinated expenditures."

13. For more extensive information about the reforms and the changes they underwent since, see Corrado 1996.

14. Of course, party money still might be appreciated by candidates as seed money, and party direct contributions combined with coordinated expenditures are more than any other single interest could offer a candidate directly.

15. For example, *FEC v. Massachusetts Citizens for Life, Inc.* (470 U.S. 238, 1986); *Austin v. Michigan State Chamber of Commerce* (494 U.S. 652, 1990).

16. SUN PAC also allowed corporations to form limitless numbers of PACs, each with its own $5,000 maximum individual contribution limit. The 1976 amendments to the FECA changed this by summing the total contributions across an organization's PACs and applying the statute's PAC maximum contribution amount per election to that total. So even if a corporation had thirty PACs, it could still contribute no more than $5,000 total to an individual.

17. In June 2001, the Court in *FEC v. Colorado Republican Federal Campaign Committee* (533 U.S. 431, 2001) upheld the coordinated expenditure restrictions contained in the FECA.

18. As of this writing in 2001, the fate of campaign finance reform is uncertain. We include the early twenty-first century here as a period in which the volume of discussion about reform, from 1993 on, has been extraordinary.

19. Thanks to Michael Franz for discussion of this two-by-two schema.

INDEX